COGNITIVE BEHAVIORAL THERAPY TECHNIQUES and STRATEGIES

COGNITIVE BEHAVIORAL THERAPY TECHNIQUES and STRATEGIES

Amy Wenzel, Keith S. Dobson, and Pamela A. Hays

American Psychological Association • Washington, DC

Published by
American Psychological Association
750 First Street, NE
Washington, DC 20002
www.apa.org

To order
APA Order Department
P.O. Box 92984
Washington, DC 20090-2984
Tel: (800) 374-2721; Direct: (202) 336-5510
Fax: (202) 336-5502; TDD/TTY: (202) 336-6123
Online: www.apa.org/pubs/books
E-mail: order@apa.org

In the U.K., Europe, Africa, and the Middle East, copies may be ordered from
American Psychological Association
3 Henrietta Street
Covent Garden, London
WC2E 8LU England

Typeset in Meridien by Circle Graphics, Inc., Columbia, MD

Printer: Bang Printing, Brainerd, MN
Cover Designer: Mercury Publishing Services, Inc., Rockville, MD

The opinions and statements published are the responsibility of the authors, and such opinions and statements do not necessarily represent the policies of the American Psychological Association.

Library of Congress Cataloging-in-Publication Data

Names: Wenzel, Amy, author. | Dobson, Keith S., author. | Hays, Pamela A.,
  author. | American Psychological Association, issuing body.
Title: Cognitive behavioral therapy techniques and strategies / Amy Wenzel,
  Keith S. Dobson, Pamela A. Hays.
Description: First edition. | Washington, DC : American Psychological
  Association, [2016] | Includes bibliographical references and index.
Identifiers: LCCN 2015045532 | ISBN 9781433822377 | ISBN 1433822377
Subjects: | MESH: Cognitive Therapy—methods.
Classification: LCC RC489.C63 | NLM WM 425.5.C6 | DDC 616.89/1425—dc23 LC record available
at http://lccn.loc.gov/2015045532

British Library Cataloguing-in-Publication Data
A CIP record is available from the British Library.

Printed in the United States of America
First Edition

http://dx.doi.org/10.1037/14936-000

Contents

Acknowledgments

We thank the American Psychological Association (APA) for the opportunity to provide this volume on cognitive behavioral therapy (CBT). For some of us, this book began through the invitation of Dr. Jon Carlson to participate in his video productions related to models of psychotherapy. This work was then advanced by Ed Meidenbauer's suggestion of a series of APA videos that presented vignettes depicting various techniques and strategies delivered by cognitive behavioral therapists over the course of treatment. We all met each other and participated in the resulting Cognitive Behavioral Therapy Techniques and Strategies series (see http://www.apa.org/pubs/videos) in which we selected samples of our own work to demonstrate the typical practice of CBT and joined together for stimulating round-table discussion. While producing that video series, it became clear that a companion text would be an excellent idea, and we have been happy to work with Susan Reynolds from APA in the production of this volume.

Of course, no single work can stand alone. We have had the privilege during our careers to work with a large number of world-class cognitive behavioral therapists, to read their works, to watch them in clinical action, and to discuss their various ideas and innovations. Aspects of many of the ideas and methods that are presented in this book can be found in a wide range of other resources, and we acknowledge the immense amount of effort and thoughtfulness that has been put into the development of the rich and diverse field of CBT.

Finally, we must acknowledge that advances in CBT rest on the openness, trust, and hard work of our clients. We could not have helped to build the methods that are described in this book unless large numbers of people, in the

first place, were in need of therapy, and in the second place, embraced
and responded well to the practice of CBT. We therefore want to acknowledge the significant role that our clients have played in the development of the ideas described in this volume. Ultimately, the value of this
volume will be determined by the clinical utility of the material that
we have presented. We hope that this book is well received in this
regard.

COGNITIVE
BEHAVIORAL
THERAPY
TECHNIQUES
and STRATEGIES

Introduction

Cognitive behavioral therapy (CBT) is a rich, complex, and evolving model of treatment that has been developed for and applied to a wide range of mental health and physical problems and disorders. From its early days in the 1970s, CBT has grown to become one of the preeminent models of psychotherapy, and it is widely distributed and used around the globe. Specific forms of CBT have been recognized as evidence-based treatments for a vast array of disorders, from organizations as wide ranging as the American Psychiatric Association, the Australian Psychological Association, the British National Institute for Clinical Excellence, and many others in many parts of the world.

This volume was written to elucidate and portray some of the key principles and therapeutic processes that are practiced by effective cognitive behavioral therapists. The organization of this book roughly follows the temporal sequence of a typical CBT application in that we begin with a discussion of the usual ways that we think broadly about the field and

http://dx.doi.org/10.1037/14936-001
Cognitive Behavioral Therapy Techniques and Strategies, by A. Wenzel, K. S. Dobson, and P. A. Hays
Copyright © 2016 by the American Psychological Association. All rights reserved.

3

then conceptualize the cognitive behavioral approach to psychotherapy. We follow this introduction with a series of chapters that discuss issues related to assessment and conceptualization of clients within CBT, typical early behavioral and problem-solving strategies, interventions that focus on both situation-specific automatic thoughts and underlying beliefs, and the processes used to end successful CBT and reduce the risk of relapse or recurrence of problems. Throughout this volume, we use three anonymized and partly fictionalized cases to provide illustrative examples of the types of in-session interactions that cognitive behavioral therapists and their clients may have, and we offer our insights and suggestions related to these cases. These three cases were chosen carefully because they portray clients with different presenting problems, unique combinations of individual-difference characteristics, and several relationship issues that could be illustrated through the dialogue that was presented.

In this introductory chapter, we provide a context for the later parts of the book, as we present some of the history related to the family of cognitive behavioral therapies. We also discuss the issues associated with foci on both therapy change and therapy process that take place within this treatment model. Finally, we conclude this introduction with a preview the following chapters, so that the reader knows what to expect.

Early CBT

Although CBT continues to evolve, most individuals see the foundation of the approach in one of two domains. For some, CBT grew from its allied field of behavior therapy. By the 1970s, behavior therapy had begun to move beyond an explicit and limited focus on observable behavior to a broader approach that included conceptions related to internal cognitions and emotions. For example, social learning theory (Bandura, 1986) recognized that when children learn a new behavior, they have to observe a model, internalize the actions of that model, and then be able to replicate the observed behavior in themselves. This complex series of acts related to observation, recognition, and planning are all cognitive activities; thus, cognitive processes played a central role in the social learning approach. Research that focused on the process of delay of gratification similarly invoked the idea that children could maintain a cognitive representation of the gratification (i.e., positive reinforcer) that they were going to obtain even as they engaged in the behavior that would eventually lead to the reinforcement. On the basis of these ideas, the field of *cognitive behavior modification* (Mahoney, 1974; Meichenbaum, 1977) began, which set the stage for *cognitive behavioral therapy*. Applications to issues such as anxiety disorders quickly evolved, and it appeared that cognitive behavior modification and social learning therapy would become movements in their own right.

The other major innovation in the 1970s that led to the development of CBT was more revolutionary than that seen in behavior therapy. Early theorists in what would become the field of CBT, such as Albert Ellis and Aaron T. Beck, were initially trained in psychoanalysis and in that training had an emphasis on early experience, unconscious process, and personality dynamics. Both theorists, however, recognized that many aspects of psychodynamic theory did not appear to contribute to significant change in psychotherapy, and they both articulated a more parsimonious and, some might argue, a more simplistic view of human dynamics in behavior change. For example, both suggested that people's beliefs affected the manner in which they viewed the world and that it was their beliefs and construal of events that was in fact more important in the ultimate response to life's circumstances than the circumstances themselves. Predicated on this assumption, both theorists developed models in which cognitive assessment and cognitive change became the pivotal point for later behavioral adaptation and emotional success. *Rational emotive therapy*, as it was called (Ellis & Whiteley, 1979), and *cognitive therapy* (A. T. Beck, 1970) eventually emerged as well developed psychotherapies that became the focus of training, research, and practice.

Since the early evolution of cognitive behavioral therapies, many other approaches have joined their ranks (K. S. Dobson & Dozois, 2009). It is now recognized that the cognitive behavioral therapies rest on several basic tenets, including the ideas that (a) cognition mediates the relation between activating events or stressors and the reactions to those stressors, (b) cognitions are not unconscious but can be monitored with training and the proper technology, and (c) systematic changes to cognition can lead to planned therapeutic outcomes.

The field of CBT, then, can be said to emerge sometime in the mid-1970s. Two additional phenomena conspired to significantly affect the long-term growth and impact of CBTs in the overall field of psychotherapy. The first was the acceptance by cognitive behavioral clinicians and theorists that clinical research methodologies could be used to evaluate the outcomes of CBT. Beginning in the 1970s, and continuing significantly throughout the next two decades, a large number of open trials, simple comparative studies, and randomized controlled trials were conducted with CBT protocols for a large number of clinical disorders. This work was significantly enhanced by the ability of CBT developers to enunciate the principles and techniques that were incorporated in treatment. Furthermore, the fact that many of the CBT protocols were short term in nature made them reasonably well suited to being written as treatment manuals.

The second factor that affected CBT's impact in the overall field of psychotherapy, and one that has been somewhat underrecognized, was the evolution of the diagnostic process itself. The *Diagnostic and Statistical Manual of Mental Disorders* (*DSM*) published by the American Psychiatric Association forms the basis for much clinical research in the field of clinical psychology and psychiatry. The third edition of the *DSM* in 1980 (*DSM–III*; American Psychiatric Association) was a significant departure from its predecessors in that it removed much of the theoretical architecture seen in earlier editions and focused on a descriptive account of psychopathology. This movement to descriptive psychopathology allowed clinicians to develop manuals that could target the specific symptoms and syndromes described in the *DSM*. Thus, it was just as CBT was beginning to develop that this change in psychopathology and diagnosis further enhanced the ability to write specific treatment manuals based on the diagnoses found in the *DSM–III*.

In part because of the preceding two factors, and of course propelled by the positive results from clinical trials that began to emerge, the field of CBT exploded in the latter part of the 1990s and into the early part of the current century. By the early 2000s, meta-analyses were being published that summarized the large numbers of individual trials and that generally documented the significant benefits of CBT for a wide range of both mental health and physical conditions. Although there are certainly limitations to the extent to which one can make this claim, it can be generally claimed that CBT "works" for a wide variety of disorders and that CBT is generally an evidence-based approach to psychotherapy. Thus, when the field began to identify the principles for evidence-based practice (Chambless et al., 1996), it is not surprising that CBT figured predominantly among the therapies that were identified.

Developments Within CBT

As discussed in this section, the field of CBT has grown dramatically since its inception. This growth has taken two primary directions. One of these is related to a more complete understanding of the applicability of the model through the development and evaluation of variants of CBT in a wide range of clinical populations, sometimes as a stand-alone treatment but also integrated with other treatments (e.g., medications), and in diverse settings (e.g., research and clinical settings, with various cultural populations). The second focus has been the effort to understand the mechanisms of change associated with CBT. This focus has included in-depth studies of the predictors of more and less successful outcomes, therapist behaviors associated with change, and aspects of the therapeutic relationship. Each of these areas is briefly discussed here.

THE FOCUS ON CHANGE

The earliest outcome trials for CBT focused on relatively specific disorders, and research trials at that time often included relatively homogeneous samples of clients and relatively more exclusion criteria than later trials. This focus on internal validity was a natural result of the desire to demonstrate that CBT had strong treatment effects, and it generally was a success in this respect. At the same time, the focus on internal validity in *efficacy* trials led to questions about the generalizability of the results from these trials to actual practice in the clinic. As a result, several researchers began to conduct what are now referred to as *effectiveness* trials to determine whether the results from more restrictive research clinical trials could be replicated in the "real world" (Nathan, Stuart, & Dolan, 2000). Generally speaking, these results were favorable, and so it became the case that treatment manuals were increasingly applied in clinical contexts.

Another issue with respect to the early development of CBT, also related to the use of randomized controlled trials with significant numbers of exclusion criteria in research contexts, was the extent to which trial results generalized to diverse populations. For example, it was noted that some of the early trials had relatively homogeneous cultural groups, and so the extent to which results might apply to other cultural groups was naturally questioned. As a result of this query, several investigators began to develop culturally adapted versions of CBT for specific populations. As one example, an adapted CBT for religiously oriented people with depression was tested and demonstrated significant positive results (Propst, Ostrom, Watkins, Dean, & Mashburn, 1992). Ricardo Muñoz and his colleagues also adapted treatments for depression with individuals of Latino heritage and demonstrated that treatment results could be found in this population (Muñoz & Mendelson, 2005). Moreover, as the success of CBT grew, it was perhaps natural that investigators would start to apply these treatments in other countries. Adaptations of CBT now exist for a wide variety of cultural, religious, ethnic, and other groups, and it is generally recognized that an important part of the skillful application of CBT involves a consideration of diversity (Naeem & Kingdon, 2012).

One particular method that has been developed to assist with the transportability and dissemination of CBT to diverse contexts is that of *benchmarking*. Benchmarking takes place when an investigator compares his or her results to those of a standard treatment. Benchmarking can take place within a given country (Wade, Treat, & Stuart, 1998; Weersing & Weisz, 2002) and across people who vary on diverse characteristics, but it can also be applied across cultures and countries to determine the extent to which the results of various trials have similar or different results (Spilka & Dobson, 2015). There has been a significant effort in recent years to establish a science of dissemination (McHugh & Barlow, 2010) as a practice that respects both the tenets of CBT and its established principles and that also recognizes and adapts to the unique characteristics in which CBT may be applied. These issues of cultural adaptation and diverse application are further discussed in this volume and in other sources.

Not surprisingly, and especially in light of the significant attention shown for CBT in the research literature, clinicians who espoused other theoretical models raised concerns about the movement in the field. They suggested that the short-term nature of CBT, the manualized nature of the treatments, the reliance on *DSM* diagnoses, and other features significantly advantaged CBT in the field of psychotherapy outcome. They also suggested that some of the nonspecific and relationship factors in psychotherapy were being underrecognized because of the manualized nature of CBT. The APA Presidential Task Force on Evidence-Based Practice (2006) served as a reminder that other factors in psychotherapy than the treatment techniques also contribute significantly to clinical outcome (Castonguay & Beutler, 2006). Thus, such factors as the therapeutic alliance, therapist empathy and genuineness, and other features of psychotherapy were given their proper recognition in the field.

Another development in the field of CBT resulted from comparative analyses of the large number of treatment manuals that had been written. By the early part of the current century, it became clear that certain general principles were being used across specific diagnoses, especially in the area of the treatment of anxiety disorders. Some researchers, such as David Barlow and colleagues, suggested that transdiagnostic models of change were possible, and efforts were made to identify transdiagnostic factors in psychotherapy in general, and CBT in particular (Barlow et al., 2011). Indeed, there have been recent studies to examine the efficacy of transdiagnostic treatments, and preliminary data suggest that these treatments are approximately as effective as specific treatment manuals for specific disorders (Farchione et al., 2012).

THE FOCUS ON PROCESS

In addition to the many developments in the outcome literature, a number of clinicians and researchers have also focused on the processes associated with CBT. This work has taken several directions. For example, some researchers have used outcome studies as the framework to study predictors of outcome or the therapy processes associated with better and worse treatment success. It is relatively easy to assess clients and therapists on a wide variety of dimensions and examine the degree to which these variables predict clinical outcome. In this regard, it is now fairly safe to conclude that client predictors of better outcome in CBT include later onset of the disorder, a less chronic disorder, and lower problem severity at the outset of treatment (Epp & Dobson, 2010). In some respects, however, these general predictors are not surprising, and they also seem to be predictors of outcome for other treatments as well. Thus, in addition to general predictors, there have been some studies that have examined differential client predictors of outcome. Such studies are relatively fewer in number, however, because this type of research requires at least two active treatments in the research study, and they often fail to identify differential predictors.

Studies of therapist predictors of outcome have been relatively uncommon in the field of CBT. Some studies have examined variables such as therapist gender and age as predictors, but they often fail to find a significant effect. In some respects, the failure of therapists' individual differences to predict outcome is a positive feature of the CBT because the implication could be taken that this type of therapy can be applied by a broad range of clinicians. One therapist variable that has been studied as a predictor and does have a modest association with outcome is therapist competency, but this relation has not been observed in all studies, suggesting either that it is not a robust predictor of outcome, or its measurement is not ideal (Webb, DeRubeis, & Barber, 2010).

Some researchers have examined therapy process factors in the context of clinical trials. For example, with repeated assessment of potential treatment mediators, it is possible to demonstrate whether certain changes precede or follow others in the clinical course. As one notable example of this type of research, DeRubeis and Feeley (1990) examined the association between general and specific treatment methods in CBT for depression across several time points in treatment and demonstrated that early change in depression was predicted by specific treatment methods, which in turn predicted enhanced therapy alliance, which then combined to predict better outcome (see also Feeley, DeRubeis, & Gelfand, 1999). As another example, in a reanalysis of a CBT trial for depression, Tang, DeRubeis, Hollon, Amsterdam, and Shelton (2007) revealed a pattern they termed a *sudden gain*, which consisted of a fairly rapid reduction in symptomatology from one session to the next, followed by relatively stable better functioning. This pattern of change was associated with better long-term outcomes in CBT for depression, relative to more slow and steady change in symptoms.

Another type of process research involves ratings of therapy sessions and the examination of factors that are associated with change. The compilation of Kazantzis and L'Abate (2007), for example, examined the relation between homework exercise and outcome in psychotherapy generally, and several of the chapters in their volume attest to the importance of homework in CBT in particular. A forthcoming volume (Kazantzis, Dattilio, & Dobson, in press) examines the therapeutic relationship in CBT and draws heavily on process studies of the relationship mechanisms that lead to an enhanced therapeutic alliance and other positive features of the relationship that are associated with better clinical outcome in CBT.

A number of authors have elaborated one of more specific process issues in CBT, examined these issues, and generated implications for clinical practice. Examples of this type of work include the examination of behavioral interventions in CBT (Farmer & Chapman, 2008), the assessment and management of resistance in CBT (Leahy, 2001), and the integration of imagery into CBT (Hackmann, Bennett-Levy, & Holmes, 2011). Other authors have developed models for the management of more general process issues, such as the applications of CBT for challenging problems (J. S. Beck, 2005), strategic decision making in the process of CBT (Wenzel, 2013), and CBT with diverse cultures (Hays & Iwamasa, 2006; Naeem & Kingdon, 2012). Often, this latter type of work draws on clinical cases and illustrations, but it adds considerable depth to the literature and often identifies areas for further theory development and research investigations.

In summary, the field of CBT is now complex and mature. We know much about the conditions for which CBT is effective, its relative efficacy in a number of comparison therapies, the outcomes associated with its clinical practice, a wide variety of predictors of outcome, and the processes associated with sound clinical practice. One of the signal strengths of the CBT movement has been its integration with research studies and the development of a strong foundation of evidence. It is therefore not surprising that CBT is often at the forefront of discussions about evidence-based practice.

The Current Volume

This book has the advantage of the rich and developing field of CBT, as well as the knowledge and experience of three scientist–practitioners who regularly deliver CBT to clients, train clinicians to be competent to practice CBT, and contribute scholarship that advances the field. We are at a phase in the development of the field in which we can make confident statements about a wide variety of principles and methods that generally have benefit across a wide range of populations and problems.

For example, there is now considerable evidence that early success in CBT homework is associated with early change, which in turn relates to improved therapeutic alliance and that all contribute to an ongoing positive association with more successful long-term outcome (Kazantzis, Whittington, & Dattilio, 2010). There is also consistent evidence that a strong therapeutic alliance, regardless of the extent of homework completion, is a significant predictor of positive outcome in CBT (Webb et al., 2011). We also know that the ability to engage in case conceptualization is a predictor of outcome and that consistency in case conceptualization is a skill that can be developed over time (Kuyken, Fothergill, Musa, & Chadwick, 2005). These issues are highlighted here because none of them deals particularly with the techniques of treatment, but rather they all focus on the process of care that is provided. One of the common ideas associated with CBT is that it is exclusively focused on treatment techniques, to the exclusion or diminishment of therapy process, but as the current volume demonstrates, this idea is a myth (D. Dobson & Dobson, 2009).

The current volume demonstrates broad principles related to CBT that an effective cognitive behavioral therapist must learn and flexibly practice with his or her varied clients. The first chapter in the book highlights the importance of case conceptualization and the model that is used to understand problems from a cognitive behavioral perspective. In this chapter, we discuss the process of psychological assessment, including the diagnostic interview, case review, and formal psychometric evaluation but also the way in which all of the assembled information combines to provide an overall evaluation of the client in the form of a cognitive case conceptualization. This case conceptualization is in many respects the heart of CBT because it is the case conceptualization that drives the choice of techniques that the therapist will deploy, and even aspects of the manner in which the therapist relates to the client (Kuyken, Padesky, & Dudley, 2008; Persons, 2008).

An important feature of CBT is that it is relatively efficient and focused. Novice cognitive behavioral therapists learn how to use their time well through a variety of structuring methods, as described in Chapter 2. For example, there is a typical beginning phase within a CBT session in which the therapist gathers brief assessment information about the client's experience in the past week or since the last appointment, any current problems or concerns, the ongoing issues that are relevant from previous sessions of therapy, and any particular methods that the therapist wants to introduce into the current session. All of this information feeds into an agenda, or list of topics that the therapist and client will address during the ensuing session. These topics are then engaged in one by one, and ideally as each topic is concluded, there is some idea about homework or practical exercises that will take the ideas expressed in therapy back into the client's day-to-day life to provide a practical application of the therapy discussion. Finally, the last part of a CBT session includes a review of the session, a review of the exercises that the client has agreed to do, and feedback about the session. This relatively structured format is something that can be learned relatively easily by novice therapists but that, in practice, is a complex set of skills to use seamlessly and with good social skill. Therefore, we spend some time talking about the flexible use of session structure in CBT to portray the nuanced and dynamic way that session structure is applied in practice.

Following our discussion of session structure, we also consider some of the major behavioral strategies that are used in the context of CBT. As noted previously, there is almost always an emphasis on the development of "real-life" applications of the therapy work, and behavioral strategies are a natural extension of therapy dialogue. That said, the nature of behavioral techniques is highly variable and needs to be tied to the case conceptualization. Although certain behavioral exercises are typical in various disorders (e.g., exposure to a feared social situation in social anxiety disorder, behavioral scheduling for individuals with depression or avoidance), the exact nature of those exercises relies on the cognitive behavioral therapist's sympathetic, collaborative, and complete understanding of the client's clinical presentation.

Although a common perception of CBT is that it implies that clients' problems are "all in the head," nothing can be further from the truth. Cognitive behavioral therapists recognize that their clients face real-world problems and that problem solving must be an important part of helping clients. Because of this understanding, cognitive behavioral therapists will typically assess the life problems each client faces, evaluate his or her past efforts to cope with these problems, assess his or her skills at problem identification and solution, and possibly engage in training new problem-solving skills so that they can be effectively applied in the client's life. These skills are described in Chapter 3. In many instances, clients only come from therapy when they have exhausted their current ability to deal with problems and need the help of a professional. As such, it is only natural that cognitive behavioral therapists will assist clients with this problem-solving focus. Often, working on concrete problems also involves the development of behavioral skills, the practice of these skills in therapy, and the translation of skills developed in the therapy context to the real world, so homework and practice are common features of problem solution.

In addition to problem-solving strategies, cognitive behavioral therapists recognize that some of the distress that clients experience is a result of particular patterns of thinking, and in some cases the underlying beliefs that clients hold about themselves, their world, or individuals in their lives. As such, a significant portion of typical CBT cases includes the assessment of clients' thinking, in terms of both the particular situations that they face and their general ways of approaching their lives. Two chapters in the current volume focus on cognitive interventions. The first of these, Chapter 4, examines the particular ways in which a client's situation-specific thoughts can be either distorted or simply unhelpful. Techniques to address distorted thinking focus on the evaluation of evidence that supports or does not support particular thoughts and the development of more accurate ways for clients to view their life circumstances. In contrast, cognitive interventions can also focus on unhelpful thinking, regardless of its evidence base. Techniques that can be used in this regard include encouraging clients to be more compassionate or caring toward themselves, imagining what a friend might say, or simply evaluating how helpful it is to be focused on a negative thought in a given situation. Examples of how these interventions can be applied with a variety of case studies are elucidated so that the reader can appreciate the strategy from both a theoretical and a practical perspective.

Chapter 5 then considers beliefs that can undergird negative thinking patterns and habits. Strategies to identify unhelpful underlying beliefs are discussed, and a variety of intervention methods are further described and illustrated with case studies. Cognitive behavioral therapists generally believe that it is the identification and modification of negative underlying beliefs that results in the most complete reduction of problems for the client's current problems and helps to reduce the likelihood of problems in the future. As such, most cognitive behavioral therapists will spend several sessions working at the level of underlying beliefs to try to obtain these therapeutic benefits.

Chapter 6 discusses the ways in which a cognitive behavioral therapist will attempt to complete the therapy process. CBT is generally an educational process, and as such, it is expected that the client will develop a series of skills, insights, and strategies that he or she can apply in the future if problems recur. To consolidate this level of understanding, it is typical that the therapist will encourage clients to reflect on the therapy process toward the end of treatment, to write down the major conceptions and strategies that they have learned over the course of therapy, and to plan for possible future stressors or challenging situations. Ideally, clients will leave with a relapse prevention plan that will help them cope with difficult situations that may occur in the future. That said, cognitive behavioral therapists recognize that not all difficulties can be anticipated, that skills may erode over time, and that sometimes it is simply a good idea to engage in a "tune-up" of skills that were previously learned. As such, cognitive behavioral therapists generally do not think about terminating the therapeutic relationship so much as closing a particular chapter, with the recognition that it may be necessary to open the next chapter if the client would benefit from future treatment.

Throughout this book, we attempt to highlight that CBT is a contextually driven and flexible treatment model. Although the essence of CBT theory should be respected across all cases, the particular skills and techniques that are practiced must make sense in the context of clients' lives and their particular struggles. CBT can be formally adapted to specific cultures (Naeem & Kingdon, 2012), but every case is recognized as unique. As such, we have incorporated a chapter (Chapter 7) on culturally responsive CBT that highlights the many diverse ways in which clients present and the wide range of diversity considerations in which an effective cognitive behavioral therapist must engage (Hays & Iwamasa, 2006). This chapter highlights the ADDRESSING formulation for the consideration of diversity characteristics (Hays, 2016), through which we encourage all readers to consider when they work with their clientele.

In contrast to the early days of CBT, the contemporary practice of CBT is complex and diverse. There now exist a large number of treatment manuals for many specific disorders, volumes that deal with nondiagnostic and transdiagnostic issues in the context of CBT, as well as a large number of books that deal with nonspecific treatment factors in psychotherapy such as homework, the therapeutic alliance, and other issues that cut across all models of psychotherapy. The field continues to evolve through the consideration and incorporation of treatment methods from other theoretical models, including mindfulness- and compassion-based interventions (Cayoun, 2011), acceptance-oriented methods (Hayes, Strosahl, & Wilson, 2011), and emotion-based models and therapy strategies (Leahy, 2015). This significant growth of the field adds to the clinical sophistication through which cognitive behavioral therapists can approach their clients but, at the same time, can create some conceptual confusion, and certainly some technical difficulty for the novice cognitive behavioral therapist.

We have distilled some of the essential treatment methods seen in CBT in this volume. We have also used hypothetical cases to illustrate some of the major methods that are discussed and to make the theoretical discussion as "real" as possible. This volume was developed as a companion to a DVD series that has also been published by the American Psychological Association press. If the reader is interested, we strongly recommend that the various chapters encompassed in this book should be read alongside the viewing and discussion of the corresponding DVD for each chapter. Through the consideration of both this written work and that DVD series, we believe that the interested therapist will get the most benefit and come away with the richest possible understanding of the various ideas and methods described in this volume.

Assessment and Case Conceptualization

1

A ssessment is the process through which a mental health professional gathers, evaluates, and integrates information about the client to arrive at a diagnosis of a mental health disorder and a conceptualization of his or her clinical presentation. *Information gathering* means that the mental health professional acquires "data" to develop a thorough understanding of the client's current and past life circumstances, stressors, strengths, and reasons for seeking treatment. As is described in more detail in the next section, data collection can be formal, such as through the administration of a well-validated psychological test, or informal, such as through a free-flowing conversation with the client. *Evaluation* means that the mental health professional "analyzes" the information that he or she gathered about the client to gain an understanding of the client's clinical presentation. For example, evaluation occurs when the mental health professional compares the client's score on a psychological test with normative scores of people representative of the general population. *Integration* means

http://dx.doi.org/10.1037/14936-002
Cognitive Behavioral Therapy Techniques and Strategies, by A. Wenzel, K. S. Dobson, and P. A. Hays

that the mental health professional incorporates data gathered and evaluated from several sources to draw conclusions about the client's clinical presentation.

In many instances, an important conclusion that is drawn is the diagnosis of the mental health disorder for which the client meets criteria. However, conclusions from psychological assessment are not limited to a focus on a diagnosis of a mental health disorder. Psychological assessment also allows mental health professionals to determine (a) clients' current and past levels of functioning, (b) stressors that trigger symptoms of mental health disorders and the helpful and unhelpful ways in which clients cope with those stressors, (c) factors that make clients vulnerable to experience symptoms of mental health disorders in times of stress, and (d) factors that contribute to resilience in times of stress.

Cognitive behavioral therapists rely heavily on assessment. They use assessment to develop a *case conceptualization*, or an understanding of the client's clinical presentation in light of the cognitive behavioral model (described later in the chapter). In a typical clinical practice, it is rare that clients present with a straightforward clinical presentation, such that they meet diagnostic criteria for only one mental health disorder for which there is an empirically supported treatment protocol. Some clients meet diagnostic criteria for two or more mental health disorders; others meet criteria for one mental health disorder but have symptoms associated with an array of other mental health disorders; still others meet criteria for a mental health disorder but have other issues that require a focus in treatment, such as a medical problem such as cancer or a behavioral problem like procrastination. A detailed case conceptualization helps the therapist to understand the manner in which the pieces of their client's clinical presentation fit together to explain the etiology, maintenance, and exacerbation of the client's emotional distress, as well as to identify the most important targets of an individualized treatment package.

In this chapter, we describe ways in which cognitive behavioral therapists conduct their psychological assessment with their clients. In addition, we present the cognitive behavioral theoretical model and demonstrate the manner in which it can be used to facilitate the case conceptualization of a client's clinical presentation. Finally, we discuss ways to use the results of the psychological assessment and the case conceptualization to facilitate treatment planning and ongoing monitoring of treatment goals.

Assessment

Assessment is an integral part of cognitive behavioral therapy (CBT). The therapist and client continually assess, throughout their time together, how specific interventions are working or not working for the client.

The *initial assessment* is the portion of the assessment process that begins before therapy starts. It can vary in the ways in which it is implemented depending on the setting, the particular therapist's approach, and the client's characteristics and preferences. In many instances, cognitive behavioral therapists meet with their clients the first time their client visits the treatment setting. In these cases, therapists typically devote between one and three sessions to psychological assessment and treatment planning before beginning CBT. However, other cognitive behavioral therapists work in settings in which psychological assessment is completed by a technician before meeting with a therapist. In these cases, cognitive behavioral therapists thoroughly review the information that is given to them from the technician before meeting with the client for the first time and devote the first session to using the assessment results for the purpose of treatment planning.

Throughout the assessment process (as well as the treatment process), cognitive behavioral therapists pay close attention to the therapeutic relationship. At the same time that they are gathering, evaluating, and integrating information about the client, therapists actively seek the client's input regarding the client's conception of the problem and what has or has not helped. That is, therapists demonstrate warmth and empathy, convey respect for the client, and communicate a sense that the client's concerns are understood. Therapists take care to instill hope that clients' problems can be addressed using the cognitive behavioral framework. They check in with the client at multiple points during the process to ensure that the client understands the rationale and is on board with a particular type of test or tool that is being administered, acknowledging clients' opinions and developing a collaborative working relationship. If the client expresses a preference to focus on something different than that on which the therapist is focusing, therapists almost always comply with this wish. Consider the following example with Shane, a 34-year-old single man of mixed race who presented for his first visit with a cognitive behavioral therapist.

> Shane was referred by a psychiatrist who was a close colleague of the cognitive behavioral therapist. The psychiatrist indicated that Shane had seen several psychotherapists in the past and that his current psychotherapist believed that it was in his best interest to transfer to someone else because she felt "stuck" with Shane. The psychiatrist also acknowledged that Shane was hopeless about treatment and was ambivalent about starting with a new psychotherapist.
>
> Shane arrived for his appointment 15 minutes late and presented with guardedness and hostility. The cognitive behavioral therapist gave Shane a warm welcome, indicating that she was pleased to be working with him and that, on the basis of the information from the psychiatrist, she believed that she could be helpful. She asked what he wanted to accomplish in the first visit, to which he responded in a dejected manner,

"I don't know." She then asked permission to share with him how she typically works with clients, such that she conducts a psychological assessment over the course of one to three visits and works collaboratively with her clients to develop a treatment plan. Shane passively agreed to this plan by nodding his head. As the session progressed, the cognitive behavioral therapist was pleasantly surprised that Shane began to open up and spontaneously describe his current life problems, so she put on hold the guided questions that she hoped to ask him to allow him space to express his concerns, feel heard and understood, and develop a sound therapeutic alliance.

During the conversation, Shane gave indications that he was struggling with symptoms of several mental health disorders. Thus, his cognitive behavioral therapist asked for permission to ask questions from a diagnostic interview to confirm the presence and severity of these disorders. Shane became agitated and responded that he felt like he was in crisis and was hoping to obtain immediately some tools that would help him to manage his emotional distress. The cognitive behavioral therapist readily complied with this request. Although she conducted some additional assessment focused on his suicide risk, they spent the rest of the session identifying and practicing behavioral coping tools.

Thus, the cognitive behavioral therapist delayed some of the assessment that she had hoped to complete with Shane. But by the end of the session, Shane left with the beginnings of a plan to manage his emotional distress and reported a small bit of optimism that CBT could be helpful for him. He scheduled another appointment with the cognitive behavioral therapist for later in the week because information she gathered from the suicide risk assessment suggested that more than one visit per week with a mental health professional was indicated. Had the cognitive behavioral therapist not responded to Shane's request to focus on coping skills, she would have run the risk that Shane would leave the session perceiving that she was not responsive to his preferences, increasing the likelihood that he would discontinue treatment at a time when he was at moderate risk for self-harm behavior.

TYPES OF ASSESSMENTS

Mental health professionals use many methods to conduct their psychological assessment, including (but not limited to) clinical interviews, self-report inventories, self-monitoring, behavioral observation, and collateral information. Each of these assessment methods is discussed in turn.

Clinical Interview

A *clinical interview* is a type of assessment in which a mental health professional gathers information from a client by asking questions (usually those that are open-ended) and recording the client's verbal (and, at times, nonverbal) responses. Clinical interviews range from unstructured to structured. Unstructured clinical interviews are those in which therapists ask clients to "tell their story" in any way that they see fit. In contrast, structured interviews are those in which there are prescribed questions that correspond to diagnoses of mental health disorders. In most instances, therapists who use structured clinical interviews ask a "probe" question for each diagnosis, and if the client responds affirmatively, they continue with prescribed questions that correspond to each diagnostic criterion for that mental health disorder. Therapists who use structured diagnostic interviews typically receive training and supervision on the use of these tools, and they are usually required to demonstrate that their determination of diagnoses of mental health disorder meets a standard of interrater reliability. An example of a structured clinical interview is the *Structured Clinical Interview for DSM–5 Disorders—Clinician Version* (SCID–5–CV; First, Williams, & Spitzer, 2015). Alternate forms of this structured interview are also available for researchers and for use in clinical trials.

Although not all cognitive behavioral therapists use structured clinical interviews, most ask questions to establish diagnoses of mental health disorders. They also ask questions that help put the client's current mental health disorder(s) in context, such as those that target the frequency, severity, and duration of previous episodes of mental health disorders, family history of mental health disorders, and the quantity, frequency, and duration of alcohol and drug use. Cognitive behavioral therapists ask their clients questions about the stressors and hassles that seem to worsen the symptoms of their mental health disorder, as well as questions about aspects of their lives that seem to lessen the impact of symptoms associated with those disorders. They ask about the manner in which their clients cope with the stress and the symptoms of their mental health disorder, both adaptive and maladaptive.

In addition, cognitive behavioral therapists ask questions about many other areas of clients' lives. They ask about current and past physical health and medical problems, as well as prescription medications (both psychotropic and nonpsychotropic) that the client is currently taking. They get a sense of the client's daily life by asking about his or her employment status, romantic relationship status, living situation, social support network, responsibilities, recreational pursuits, exercise, and involvement in or practice of religious or spiritual traditions and activities. They ask about the client's family of origin, taking care to understand what the client's home life was like while he or she was growing up, the quality of the relationships with his or her parents and siblings during childhood and adolescence, and the current quality of those relationships. They ask about the client's educational background, learning how far the client went in school and the types of experiences the client had in school. They ask about the client's past peer relationships, including positive experiences with close friends as well as negative experiences in which the client perceived that he or she was rejected, teased, or bullied. They ask about experiences of physical, sexual, and emotional abuse. They ask about the client's cultural background and the ways in which the family's culture, race, ethnicity, religion, and traditions affected his or life and worldview. They also ask clients to describe any other key life experiences, positive or negative, that had a significant impact on them or shaped the manner in which they view themselves or the world today.

During the first visit they have with a client, cognitive behavioral therapists conduct a suicide risk assessment to determine the client's level of risk for engaging in suicidal behavior and determining the appropriate level of care. Although some clients may be reluctant to answer such questions, suicide risk assessments are essential to ensure that at-risk clients are receiving the necessary care to reduce the likelihood that they will engage in suicidal behavior. When therapists conduct suicide risk assessments, they ask clients about the frequency, intensity, and duration of suicidal ideation (i.e., thoughts and images about suicide), their intent to act on any suicidal ideation, plans they have made to harm themselves, and whether they have access to lethal means. In addition, they assess for factors that research has shown to put people at increased risk for engaging in suicidal behavior (e.g., social isolation, family history of suicide) and factors that research has shown to put people at decreased risk for engaging in suicidal behavior, or those that are protective (e.g., being a parent). Cognitive behavioral therapists then assimilate the information obtained from the suicide risk assessment to determine whether a client is at minimal, moderate, or imminent risk of suicidal behavior (for further discussion, see Wenzel, Brown, & Beck, 2009). Minimal risk signifies that the client can be seen on an outpatient basis as needed; moderate risk signifies that monitoring is necessary beyond weekly outpatient psychotherapy visits (e.g., psychotherapy sessions two or three times a week; telephone check-ins between sessions; involvement of family members). Imminent risk signifies that the client is likely to make a suicide attempt within 24 to 48 hours of the time of the risk assessment and that hospitalization is indicated.

As can be seen in this discussion, the information obtained from a clinical interview is rich and varied, representing both the client's current life situation as well as key information from his or her past. No two clinicians will conduct clinical interviews in an identical manner (unless they only administer a structured clinical interview). Cognitive behavioral therapists typically asked guided questions to obtain this information, such that they first ask general questions to probe each of these areas, and they then ask specific follow-up questions as appropriate that are tailored to the responses that the client supplied. Moreover, they ask additional questions that are relevant to unique clinical presentations with which clients present. For example, a cognitive behavioral therapist who works with a woman presenting with postpartum depression will ask detailed questions about her pregnancy, labor and delivery experience, and plans for child care.

Self-Report Inventories

Self-report inventories are paper-and-pencil or computer-administered measures in which clients rate aspects of their emotional, cognitive, physiological, and behavioral experiences. Thousands of self-report inventories have been developed to assess various types of psychological phenomena for both clinical and research purposes. Cognitive behavioral therapists often supplement clinical interviews with well-validated self-report inventories that assess common clinical phenomena, such as depression or anxiety. An advantage of using self-report inventories is that scores from any one client can be compared with scores from individuals representative of the general population. This allows the therapist to determine whether the client's score exceeds the cut point for a diagnosis of a mental health disorder, as well as the severity of the mental health problem that is targeted in the self-report inventory.

Cognitive behavioral therapists can use any self-report inventory that has relevance to the client's clinical presentation, provided that it has adequate psychometric properties (i.e., acceptable levels of reliability and validity). Perhaps the most common self-report inventories that are used by cognitive behavioral therapists are the Beck Scales, authored by the "father of CBT," Dr. Aaron T. Beck (see http://www.beckscales.com). The most widely known of the Beck Scales is the Beck Depression Inventory—II (BDI–II), a 21-item scale that measures symptoms corresponding to the fourth and fifth editions of the *Diagnostic and Statistical Manual of Mental Disorders* symptoms of depression (A. T. Beck, Steer, & Brown, 1996). Cognitive behavioral therapists often administer the BDI–II to clients before they begin their first session so that they have an idea of their client's depressive symptoms, as well as periodically throughout the course of treatment. Other common Beck Scales include the Beck Anxiety Inventory (A. T. Beck & Steer, 1990) that assesses physiological (e.g., heart racing) and cognitive (e.g., fear of dying) symptoms associated with anxiety and the Beck Hopelessness Scale (A. T. Beck & Steer, 1988) that assesses severity of hopelessness, a factor that can elevate a client's suicide risk.

Self-Monitoring

Self-monitoring is a type of assessment in which clients prospectively track their cognitive, behavioral, physiological, and emotional experiences in their daily lives. Clients who engage in self-monitoring make note of their experiences as they occur, eliminating the possibility that retrospective or overgeneral memory distorts their self-report. Information obtained from self-monitoring helps cognitive behavioral therapists to understand what triggers upsetting emotional reactions in their clients, specific psychological reactions associated with those triggers, and typical patterns of coping (e.g., avoidance, alcohol use). Maladaptive or otherwise unhelpful psychological reactions can be targets of treatment; conversely, evidence of adaptive or helpful psychological reactions can serve to increase clients' self-confidence that they have the ability to handle their life problems. Self-monitoring forms can be used in the service of *functional assessment*, or the identification of antecedents and consequences of problematic behavior, which can then serve as targets in treatment (e.g., Abramowitz, Deacon, & Whiteside, 2011).

Figure 1.1 is an example of a typical self-monitoring form. However, it should be acknowledged that self-monitoring is flexible, and any information that the therapist and client believe would be important to track

FIGURE 1.1

Date	Trigger	Emotion (0 = *low intensity*; 10 = *highest intensity*)	Thought	Physiological sensation (0 = *low intensity*; 10 = *highest intensity*)	Behavioral response

Sample self-monitoring form.

for the purposes of psychological assessment can be included. Moreover, the specific manner in which clients record their self-monitoring data is also flexible, as long as it is recorded somewhere rather than stored in memory. For example, there are many CBT mobile phone applications (i.e., apps) that include a self-monitoring function (e.g., MoodKit for iPhone and iPad; iPromptU for iPhone, iPad, and Android). In addition, clients can simply record their self-monitoring data in the notes function of their smartphones or tablet devices.

Behavioral Observation

Behavioral observation refers to an assessment method in which a therapist observes, firsthand, the manner in which the client responds to a trigger or stimulus for an upsetting emotional experience or maladaptive behavior or the manner in which the client lives his of her life outside of the therapist's office. Cognitive behavioral therapists can conduct behavioral observation informally or formally. Informally, they can observe the manner in which their client behaves in session and responds to them. For example, Shane's guardedness and hostility were important pieces of data that his therapist observed in their initial appointment, which shaped her case conceptualization and the manner in which she responded to him. Many therapists assimilate behavioral observations from the first visits with a client into a *Mental Status Examination*, documenting their client's appearance, attitude, behavior, mood and affect, speech, thought process, thought content, perception, cognition, insight, and judgment (Trzepacz & Baker, 1993). This information informs the diagnosis that the therapist ultimately assigns.

Behavioral observation can also be conducted in a formal manner. Therapists who conduct formal behavioral observation go into the client's natural environment (e.g., school, home) to observe the antecedents and consequences of the client's behavior. Before embarking on a formal behavioral observations, therapists typically develop operational definitions of the constructs that they are assessing. For example, if a therapist is assessing for the presence of hyperactivity, he would first define hyperactivity in observable and behavioral terms (e.g., child gets out of her seat when the teacher is instructing). When the therapist is in the client's environment and observing the client's behaviors, he might record each instance of a problematic behavior that he had previously defined, or he might indicate whether the behavior occurred within a predetermined interval (e.g., 5 minutes). When possible, the therapist will select at least two comparison individuals and monitor their behavior using the same scheme. The therapist then uses the objective data discerned from the behavioral observation to (a) substantiate that the client meets diagnostic criteria for a mental health disorder, (b) identify factors that increase or decrease the likelihood that the client engages in problematic behavior, (c) document the manner in which the client's problematic behavior is associated with life interference, and (d) identify potential targets for treatment.

Collateral Information

Collateral information is information about the client that is supplied by a family member, health care professional, teacher, or someone else who has close contact with the client and has had many opportunities to observe his or her behavior. Collateral information can be gathered in many ways. For example, parents and spouses sometimes participate in clinical interviews, either along with the client or during a separate appointment, to share their observations and views on the manner in which the client's mental health problem is affecting the client's life. Structured clinical interviews for parents have been developed to determine diagnoses of mental health disorders in children (e.g., Silverman & Albano, 2005). In addition, there are several self-report inventories assessing symptoms of mental health disorders in children that have parent and teacher versions (e.g., Achenbach 1991/2001, 2001). Cognitive behavioral therapists also solicit the records from concurrent and previous mental health providers to aid in the psychological assessment and in the development of the cognitive case conceptualization.

COURSE OF ASSESSMENT

Although the initial assessment typically occurs in the first one to three sessions of CBT, it is important to understand that the boundary between assessment and psychotherapy is fluid. During the initial course of assessment, a cognitive behavioral therapist might very well implement a therapeutic intervention to address an aversive emotional experience or behavior that is reported by the client. Moreover, assessment does not end after the first few visits with a client. Indeed, assessment is a part of every psychotherapy session that cognitive behavioral therapists have with their clients. As described in greater detail in Chapter 2, cognitive behavioral therapists typically conduct a brief mood check at the beginning of each session, such that their clients give them objective indices of their mood state in the time between sessions. Cognitive behavioral therapists also use behavioral observation, client self-report, and sometimes collateral report to determine whether the interventions that they are implementing are achieving their desired results and are helping clients meet their treatment goals. When necessary, cognitive behavioral therapists administer additional psychological tests if a new or previously undetected problem becomes apparent.

The focus on assessment is one aspect of cognitive behavioral therapy that makes it relatively unique among the psychotherapies. Cognitive behavioral therapists conduct themselves as "scientist–practitioners," bringing an empirical approach to understanding their client's clinical presentation and evaluating the course of psychotherapy. Using this approach, cognitive behavioral therapists make strategic, evidence-informed decisions as they proceed with treatment, as will be seen in the remaining chapters of this volume.

Case Conceptualization

Case conceptualization is the process through which cognitive behavioral therapists use the results from the psychological assessment to understand their client's clinical presentation in light of the cognitive behavioral model. The case conceptualization helps the cognitive behavioral therapist identify the factors that precipitated, maintain, and exacerbate the client's mental health disorder. It also points to modifiable cognitive, emotional, and behavioral factors that can be targeted in psychotherapy using strategic therapeutic interventions.

COGNITIVE BEHAVIORAL MODEL

The development of a case conceptualization requires that the cognitive behavioral therapist have a sound understanding of the cognitive behavioral model that underlies assessment and treatment. The cognitive behavioral model is often presented in two ways. The *basic* model conceptualizes the psychological factors that characterize the manner in which a person responds to a particular situation in a particular moment. This model is essential in characterizing clients' emotional reactivity and approaches to problem solving of current, present-day life challenges. The *expanded* model accounts for key life experiences that have shaped underlying cognitive and behavioral patterns, both of which affect the likelihood that a person will experience certain cognitions, emotions, behaviors, and physiological reactions in these particular situations. In other words, the basic cognitive behavioral model describes and explains the psychological reactions that a person has in a particular situation, and the expanded cognitive model provides longitudinal and sociocultural context to understand how those psychological reactions developed and were reinforced over time, as well as the ways in which these patterns are activated and exert influence in the present (cf. Kuyken, Padesky, & Dudley, 2008).

Basic Cognitive Behavioral Model

Figure 1.2 displays the basic cognitive behavioral model. According to this model, when a person is faced with a particular situation, he or she experiences cognition about the situation that is in turn associated with emotional, behavioral, and physiological reactions. *Cognition* is a broad term that can incorporate thoughts that are stated verbally in one's mind, as well as mental images, interpretations, judgments, attitudes, perceptions, and meanings. Thus, as stated in the Introduction, cognitive behavioral therapists believe that situations do not cause people to react a certain way; rather, the meaning that people make of the situations can, in large part, explain their reactions. Cognitive behavioral therapists often refer to these cognitions as *automatic thoughts* because people experience them so quickly that they often do not realize that the thoughts are present (e.g., J. S. Beck, 2011).

Notice that we are taking care not to use causal language here. It would be simplistic to say that thoughts *cause* emotional, behavioral, and physiological reactions. In Figure 1.2, there are bidirectional arrows between each of the four psychological constructs—cognition,

FIGURE 1.2

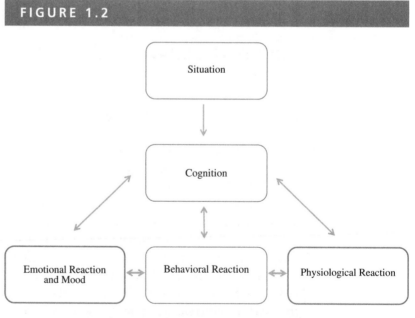

Basic cognitive behavioral model. From *Exploring Three Approaches to Psychotherapy* (p. 132), by L. S. Greenberg, N. McWilliams, and A. Wenzel, 2014, Washington, DC: American Psychological Association. Copyright 2014 by the American Psychological Association.

emotional reactions, behavioral reactions, and physiological reactions—
to account for the subjective experience of some of our clients (substan-
tiated by some empirical research), indicating that emotions, behaviors,
and physiology can affect cognition just as much as cognition can affect
them (Clore & Ortony, 2000). To shed some clinical relevance on this theoretical model, consider the case of Beth, a 52-year-old Polish American
divorced woman who presented for treatment due to stress associated
with her job as a special education teacher.

> When Beth presented for therapy, she stated, "My life is a mess."
> She described becoming overwhelmed to the point of being
> paralyzed with her job as a special education teacher at an elite
> school for children with disabilities, constantly doubting her ability
> as a teacher. She indicated that she had several "meltdowns" on
> the job in which she cried uncontrollably and left the classroom,
> leaving her assistant teacher in charge for, at times, up to an hour.
> Beth indicated that she was embarrassed by her inability to handle
> her responsibilities and believed that her colleagues thought
> poorly of her.
>
> Following a thorough assessment that included attention to
> the ways in which environmental factors might be contributing
> to Beth's difficulties, Beth's cognitive behavioral therapist helped
> her to understand that her reactions were understandable given
> the particular stressors in this environment (e.g., physical risks,
> long hours, excessive paperwork, frustrated parents and teach-
> ers) as well as in the ways in which she was viewing her ability
> to function in this stressful work environment. He asked Beth to
> identify one specific situation in which she felt overwhelmed at
> work. Beth chose to focus on an instance in which a boy with
> autism spectrum disorder became violent toward another child,
> and she did not know how to deescalate the situation. The cog-
> nitive behavioral therapist asked her what ran through her mind
> when this incident occurred. Beth recalled a slew of thoughts,
> including, "The other child is going to be seriously hurt, I will
> be accountable, and I will lose my job," and "I am a horrible
> teacher. I'm damaging these children." He then asked her what
> she felt emotionally and physiologically, as well as how she
> responded behaviorally to the situation. Beth indicated that she
> experienced a mixture of intense emotions—horror, anxiety, and
> dejection—and many physiological symptoms consistent with a
> panic attack, such as racing heart, "tunnel vision," and difficulty
> breathing. She recalled that, behaviorally, she froze for long
> enough that her assistant left what she was doing with a group
> of other children and came to her aid. Beth noted that the more
> anxious she got, the more she catastrophized about horrible
> things happening (e.g., the aggressive child causing permanent
> damage to the victim), and the less likely she was to take effec-
> tive action.
>
> Beth's cognitive behavioral therapist helped her to see that
> her emotional, physiological, and behavioral reactions were
> actually consistent with the way in which she appraised the

situation (i.e., that she was a horrible teacher who causes damage to her children and is in danger of losing her job). He also helped her to identify additional automatic thoughts that arose when she reflected on the situation (e.g., "I'm incapable of handling this job"), which were associated with further depression, anxiety, and maladaptive behavioral responses (e.g., eating lunch in the bathroom instead of sitting down for lunch with her colleagues in the teacher's lounge). As a result of this discussion, Beth developed a thorough understanding of the interrelation of her thoughts, emotions, physiological reactions, and behaviors, and she and her therapist began to identify multiple points at which she could develop alternative, and more adaptive, skills for coping.

Thus, the basic cognitive behavioral model helps therapists and clients alike make sense of what happens in situations that cause stress, anxiety, or disappointment in clients' lives. It normalizes clients' psychological experiences, allowing them to understand that their emotional, behavioral, and physiological reactions are to be expected in light of the meaning the situation held for them. It also provides a template for clients to approach future stressors and challenges from a coherent framework, supplying a guide for applying cognitive and behavioral tools to ensure that they handle these situations in an adaptive manner.

Expanded Cognitive Behavioral Model

Figure 1.3 displays the expanded cognitive behavioral model. According to this model, people have key background factors that shape both helpful and unhelpful beliefs about themselves (e.g., "I am a good person," "I am inadequate"), others ("People fundamentally have good intentions," "Others can't be trusted"), the world around them (e.g., "Beauty is all around us," "The world is a dangerous place"), and the future (e.g., "Good things will come my way," "Things will never change"). Some of those background factors are environmental in nature, such as formative experiences that occurred during childhood, adolescence, or even key times in adulthood. These formative experiences can be single instances, such as a trauma or a time when someone said something hurtful. Beth, for example, recalled receiving a failing grade in science on her report card when she was in fifth grade, and she experienced her parents' reactions as shaming and rejecting. However, formative experiences can also be related to repetitive and ongoing life circumstances such as living in poverty or in an environment where the client experiences prejudice and discrimination. For example, Shane's self-defeating thoughts developed in part out of his rejection by some White women, along with experiences of racism growing up in an upper-middle-class White community. These experiences of oppression may contribute to the development of helpful and unhelpful coping strategies, but which-

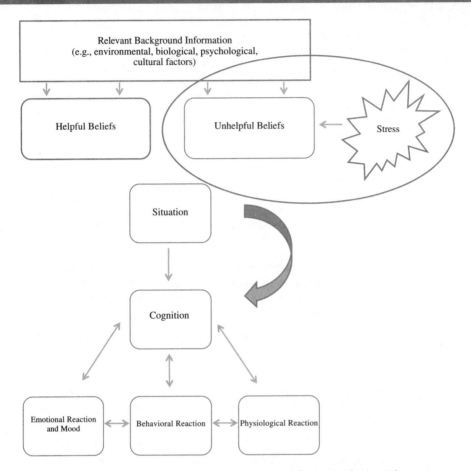

Expanded cognitive behavioral model. Adapted from *Exploring Three Approaches to Psychotherapy* (p. 135), by L. S. Greenberg, N. McWilliams, and A. Wenzel, 2014, Washington, DC: American Psychological Association. Copyright 2014 by the American Psychological Association.

ever is the case, it is important that therapists validate such experiences when the client reports them to avoid the implication that such experiences are only a matter of perception. This validation of the client's experiences does not preclude considering unhelpful beliefs that have grown out of the experiences. However, such work would be started only after the client clearly trusts and feels understood by the therapist.

At times, seemingly positive early experiences can nevertheless set the stage for the development of unhelpful beliefs that are associated with mental health disorders. Consider the case of Ajit, a 42-year-old man originally from India and now a successful businessman in the United States.

> Ajit presented for treatment with moderate to severe depression associated with the belief that he was an impostor despite an impressive resume of educational and professional achievements. In his second visit, he and his cognitive behavioral therapist agreed to devote the session to understanding key life events that shaped his beliefs and that had the potential to account for some of the depression that he was experiencing. Ajit recalled that at the end of each school year, there was a ceremony in which the most talented student in all six of his academic subjects received "prizes." When he was in fourth grade, he received all six of the prizes. Although he won prizes in subsequent years, he never again won all six, and he perceived that his father was disappointed in him for this reason. Ajit began to view himself as a "one-hit wonder." Whenever he experienced a professional success, he experienced a great deal of anxiety, wondering if this was the last time that he would accomplish something of worth and if the rest of his life would be worthless.
> Ajit's cognitive behavioral therapist recognized that his academic success was a potential source of strength and resilience. However, his negative interpretation of his father's reaction to his success contributed to Ajit's ongoing sense of failure.

In addition to environmental factors, cognitive behavioral therapists also acknowledge the biological factors at work in conceptualizing their clients' clinical presentations. For example, a family history of mental health disorders raises the possibility that a client has a substantial genetic vulnerability for emotional distress. Women who present for treatment during pregnancy or soon after childbirth may be dealing with the effects of substantial hormonal variability. Clients who report major medical problems may be experiencing mood disturbance as a result of the pathophysiology of the disease or as a side effect from the medications that they are taking.

In addition, clients may present with a host of psychological vulnerability factors that increase the likelihood that they will experience a mental health disorder. A *psychological vulnerability* is a personality trait or a pattern of cognitive, emotional, or behavioral responding that makes it difficult for people to handle challenges, stressors, disappointments, or other types of adversity. Examples include perfectionism, the intolerance of uncertainty, and poor problem-solving skills. These patterns are often heavily entrenched into a person's characteristic way of living and can be particularly challenging to overcome when a person is struggling with a mental health disorder. Shane, for example, was a person whose approach to life was characterized by impatience and an inability to delay gratification. These traits caused problems in his relationships; although he very much wanted close relationships, especially one that was romantic in nature, he expected relationships to blossom immediately after he met people, which was experienced by others as off-putting and ultimately created more distance. These traits also disrupted his relationships with previous psychotherapists because he expected his psychotherapists to have all the answers for him and quickly became frustrated when this expectation was violated.

In the past, when attention was given by cognitive behavioral therapists to environmental influences, culture was often overlooked, particularly minority cultural influences. However, as the diversity of researchers, providers, and clients increases, the importance of culture is gaining greater recognition. With all clients, it is essential that the individual's unique identity and background be considered in the case conceptualization. Failure to do so has the potential to disrupt development of a sound and collaborative therapeutic alliance. Moreover, in some instances, cognitive and behavioral patterns of responding might be viewed by the therapist as abnormal or maladaptive, when in fact they are normative for the client's family system and community. Cognitive behavioral therapists always respect the cultural beliefs that clients hold and do not push them to adopt a different set of beliefs, even if the therapist thinks that another set of beliefs would be more adaptive. Hays (2016) recommended that psychologists use the ADDRESSING framework to be aware of the multiple influences that affect clients' clinical presentations, including influences relevant to *A*ge/generation, *D*evelopmental and other *D*isabilities, *R*eligious and spiritual orientation, *E*thnic and racial identity, *S*ocioeconomic status, *S*exual orientation, *I*ndigenous heritage, *N*ational origin, and *G*ender.

The uniqueness of cultural factors affecting clients' situations is illustrated in the examples of Shane, Beth, and Ajit. Shane was part African American and part European American, and he grew up and lived in a wealthy community composed almost exclusively of White people. Shane reported many experiences of discrimination and described difficulties in finding a romantic partner in part to his sense that White women in his community would not want to be seen with a person of color. Beth was a first-generation American born to Polish parents who immigrated to the United States when they were in their early 20s. Beth described Polish culture as one that was pessimistic and focused on the negative, and she believed that this modeling influenced the way in which she viewed most events in her life. Ajit, a native of India, indicated that in his culture, it brought shame on the family if a first-born son (as he was) achieved less than his father had. His father was one of the most highly regarded surgeons in India, a position it would be impossible to "top." Ajit's negative thoughts were clearly affected by the cultural belief that being a surgeon was the highest status possible and, at the same time, contradicted by the cultural belief that he must achieve a higher status than his father.

All of these factors affect the development of beliefs that people hold about themselves, others, the world around them, and the future. Rarely do cognitive behavioral therapists encounter clients who have uniformly negative or unhelpful beliefs. As Figure 1.3 illustrates, people carry both helpful and unhelpful beliefs, and it is only in times of stress or adversity that the unhelpful beliefs are activated. In times of relative calm, the helpful, or more positive, beliefs usually predominate. Thus, this expanded cognitive behavioral model is an example of a diathesis-stress model, in that people have vulnerabilities for unhelpful or maladaptive psychological patterns that are only manifest in times of stress. For example, when Ajit landed a large business deal, he was able to experience a temporary sense of fulfillment because he recognized that he was capable and that he had a good work ethic (i.e., both helpful beliefs). However, Ajit had a low tolerance for risk and uncertainty, and when there was a slight indication that a project was not going as planned, his unhelpful beliefs were activated, and he anticipated that he would ultimately fail.

According to the renowned cognitive behavioral therapist, Dr. Judith S. Beck (2011), cognitive behavioral therapists often encounter two types of underlying beliefs in their clients. *Core beliefs* are the most fundamental beliefs that people hold. They often reflect one of three broad domains: (a) unlovability (e.g., "I am undesirable to others"), (b) helplessness (e.g., "I am trapped"), and (c) worthlessness (e.g., "I am a burden"). *Intermediate beliefs* are those that capture implicit rules and assumptions by which people live their lives. They are named as such because they are thought to stem from core beliefs but are more pervasive and persistent than situational automatic thoughts. Intermediate beliefs often take the form of "if–then" conditional assumptions. For example, Shane was characterized by the core beliefs "I'm undesirable" and "I'll be alone forever" on the basis of rejections by multiple women. His intermediate beliefs became evident when he was contemplating asking another woman out on a date, such as "If one woman rejects me, it means that no one will ever want me."

When unhelpful beliefs are activated in times of stress, the likelihood increases that people will experience negative or unhelpful automatic thoughts when they are faced with stressors, disappointment, or adversity. This, in turn, increases the likelihood of emotional distress and maladaptive behavioral reactions, such as poor self-care or making a poor choice. Continuing with the example of Shane, consider an instance in which he was trying to hold a conversation with a woman at a coffee shop, with the hope that he would feel a connection and then ask her out on a date. Because he was in the midst of a depression, his unhelpful beliefs were fully activated. When the woman with whom he was interacting looked at the clock on her smartphone (i.e., situation),

Shane immediately interpreted her behavior as evidence that she was bored and uninterested (i.e., his automatic thought). As a result, he experienced a surge of sadness as well as anger, his heart began beating quickly, and he ended the conversation abruptly, thereby ensuring that he would not go on a date with her. Had these underlying beliefs been inactive, he might not even have noticed that she looked at her smartphone, or he might have made a more benign attribution (e.g., "she just needs to know what time it is to make sure she is not late to her next appointment").

Thus, according to the expanded cognitive behavioral model, underlying beliefs shape the types of automatic thoughts experienced in any one situation. Two people can be faced with the same situation, but because they are characterized by different types of underlying beliefs, they experience very different automatic thoughts. People also develop habitual strategies to cope with their underlying beliefs, called *compensatory strategies.* Some of these strategies are adaptive behaviors that are enacted in excess so that the person is protected from the reality of the belief being realized. Because Ajit, for example, was so concerned about being a failure or a "one-hit wonder," he worked long hours and often neglected his own self-care (e.g., exercise, adequate sleep) to push himself to reach his goals.

Other compensatory strategies reinforce the underlying belief. Beth, for example, believed that she was incompetent, and she often avoided taking action when action was clearly indicated, which reinforced her notion of incompetence. In some instances, people engage in both types of compensatory strategies, as was the case with Shane, who often pursued women intensely (e.g., sending multiple text messages at a time), but then pushed them away by behaving in a socially undesirable manner. Although compensatory strategies are often behavioral in nature, they are not limited to overt behaviors that are observable by others. For example, counting, praying, and worrying are examples of cognitive compensatory strategies that have been observed in clients who are attempting to neutralize the emotional distress associated with negative automatic thoughts and unhelpful underlying beliefs.

DEVELOPMENT OF THE CASE CONCEPTUALIZATION

Cognitive behavioral therapists begin developing their case conceptualization from the minute they receive information about the client, whether it is from an initial telephone call to schedule an appointment, an intake report compiled by a staff member at their agency, or from information gathered at the first appointment. At first, cognitive behavioral therapists develop hypotheses about clients' core beliefs, intermediate beliefs, and strategies that they use to compensate for these beliefs. As they continue to meet with their clients for CBT sessions, they revise the conceptualization on the basis of the information that they are learning about their clients. Thus, the case conceptualization is not "set in stone"; rather, it is an evolving understanding of their clients' clinical presentation and background factors that can account for the clinical presentation that is refined over time, becoming richer and more intricate as therapeutic work deepens.

Cognitive behavioral therapists are cognizant of their client's case conceptualization as they are working in session with clients because they are continuously integrating information into and refining the conceptualization as their work proceeds. In addition, many cognitive behavioral therapists assimilate relevant information for the case conceptualization into a written document or computer file so that it is easily accessible. Figure 1.4 shows an example of a sample case conceptualization recording form that cognitive behavioral therapists can use for this purpose. As with the self-monitoring form, cognitive behavioral therapists need not be limited to the domains of information that are captured on this form—any type of information that is relevant to understanding the etiological, maintaining, and exacerbating factors of a client's clinical presentation can be assimilated into the case conceptualization. This particular approach to conceptualization is divided into four sections: (a) the vulnerability factors captured in the expanded cognitive behavioral model (i.e., Figure 1.3); (b) underlying beliefs, as well as compensatory strategies for coping with those beliefs; (c) stressors that have the potential to activate unhelpful beliefs; and (d) situational manifestations of unhelpful thinking and responding, corresponding to the basic cognitive behavioral model (i.e., Figure 1.2). Figure 1.5 displays the beginnings of Shane's case conceptualization, developed by his cognitive behavioral therapist over the course of his first two appointments. In this case conceptualization, she integrated information that Shane shared in his first two visits, as well as information communicated to her by the psychiatrist who referred him.

The case conceptualization is the cornerstone of CBT. It can help therapists to integrate seemingly disparate pieces of information and client experiences into a coherent framework. This is especially useful with clients who seem to present with different "crises" at the time of each visit because the conceptualization can aid the therapist in identifying the underlying themes that may account for the client's cognitive, emotional, and behavioral reactions.

The case conceptualization can also guide the therapist's response during a rupture in the therapeutic relationship. Most therapists experience ruptures as uncomfortable, making it easy to personalize the client's response to them or become angry at the client or situation. The

FIGURE 1.4

Vulnerability Factors				
Environmental:				
Biological:				
Psychological:				
Cultural:				
Beliefs				
Helpful Beliefs:				
Unhelpful Core Beliefs:				
Unhelpful Rules and Assumptions:				
Unhelpful Compensatory Strategies:				
Stressors				
Chronic Stressors:				
Acute Stressors:				
Situational Manifestations				
Situation	Automatic Thought	Emotional Reaction	Physiological Reaction	Behavioral Reaction

Sample case conceptualization document.

case conceptualization can help make the client's response to a rupture understandable in light of the factors that maintain and exacerbate his or her clinical presentation, and they can assist the therapist in identifying the psychological factors that contributed to the rupture and ways to repair them. For example, at one point during the course of CBT, Beth expressed dissatisfaction with her therapist, indicating that she perceived that her therapist was pushing her to be something that she was not. Rather than becoming defensive, the cognitive behavioral therapist realized that Beth was ambivalent about enacting solutions to problems she had addressed in therapy because of the core

FIGURE 1.5

Vulnerability Factors
Environmental: Few friends in school; bullied in middle school; many rejections by girls and women throughout his life
Biological: Family history of depression and obsessive–compulsive disorder; paternal grandfather committed suicide; maternal uncle alcoholic
Psychological: Impatience; inability to delay gratification; poor social skills; difficulty accurately inferring social cues
Cultural: Reared in affluent neighborhood consisting of mainly White families; discrimination due to being of mixed race

Beliefs
Helpful Beliefs: I'm capable (academically and professionally).
Unhelpful Core Beliefs: I'm undesirable; I'll always be alone; no one cares.
Unhelpful Rules and Assumptions: If one woman rejects me, then no one will want me; life is not worth living without a romantic partner.
Unhelpful Compensatory Strategies: Relentless pursuit of potential romantic interests; self-defeating behavior when he encounters possible problems in relationships.

Stressors
Chronic Stressors: Social isolation
Acute Stressors: None

Situational Manifestations				
Situation	Automatic Thought	Emotional Reaction	Physiological Reaction	Behavioral Reaction
Woman looks at time on her smartphone	She's bored and uninterested.	Sadness; anger	Racing heart	Abruptly ends conversation
Looking through profiles on an Internet dating site	The good ones won't want me.	Dejection	None	Doesn't attempt contact with prospects; drinks three shots
Playoff game on television	Everyone has better things to do than to watch it with me.	Depressed	Gastrointestinal distress	Doesn't reach out to friends to see if they want to watch the game

Completed case conceptualization document.

belief of incompetence and the pessimistic approach to life to which she was exposed while growing up. When Beth's cognitive behavioral therapist opened a discussion that linked what was happening in their relationship to the case conceptualization, Beth realized that her reaction to her therapist was a manifestation of the very cognitive behavioral patterns that originally brought her into treatment. Thus, what was initially a roadblock in their cognitive behavioral work turned into an important opportunity for learning through the vehicle of the case conceptualization.

Treatment Planning

A primary function of the case conceptualization is to facilitate treatment planning. The idea is that psychological factors that contribute to the etiology, maintenance, and exacerbation of mental health disorders are modifiable, so the most significant factors in the conceptualization are the ones that are identified as primary targets of treatment. As the assessment phase of a cognitive behavioral therapist's work with a client comes to a close, they move toward developing a *treatment plan* to guide their work.

Treatment plans generally consist of three components: (a) problem areas, (b) objective ways to measure progress, and (c) cognitive behavioral strategies that will be used to help clients make progress with their problem areas. Figure 1.6 displays a sample treatment plan. Problem areas are domains that the client sees as interfering with his or her functioning, quality of life, life satisfaction, or a combination of these. When asked to identify problem areas, many clients respond with vague issues such as "relationship problems" or "depression." The case conceptualization aids in delineating the specific cognitive and behavioral manifestations of the problem area that can be targeted in treatment. For example, Shane identified "problems in romantic relationships" as his most significant problem area. His therapist used the conceptualization to identify his limited social skills, difficulty detecting social cues, and inaccurate expectations for new relationships as specific manifestations of this problem area (see Figure 1.7).

Cognitive behavioral therapists measure progress toward treatment goals in as observable and measurable behaviors as possible. Shane and his therapist decided they would know that they were making progress in his problem area when he remained in conversations with women until they naturally came to a close (vs. escaping when he perceived that they were not interested), verified the assumptions that he was making about people with whom he was interacting before acting on

FIGURE 1.6

Problem Area	Manifestations of Problem Area	Indicators of Progress	Therapeutic Intervention
Problem Area #1 _____ _____ _____	1. 2. 3. 4.	1. 2. 3. 4.	1. 2. 3. 4.
Problem Area #2 _____ _____ _____	1. 2. 3. 4.	1. 2. 3. 4.	1. 2. 3. 4.
Problem Area #3 _____ _____ _____	1. 2. 3. 4.	1. 2. 3. 4.	1. 2. 3. 4.
Problem Area #4 _____ _____ _____	1. 2. 3. 4.	1. 2. 3. 4.	1. 2. 3. 4.

Sample treatment plan.

them, initiating an appropriate number of connections with potential romantic partners (vs. sending an inordinate number of text messages), and tolerating infrequent contact with potential romantic partners as their relationship was just budding.

Of course, many of these measures of progress needed further operational definition; for example, how would Shane know that a conversation was naturally coming to a close? What is an appropriate number of text messages to send a potential romantic partner? When developing treatment plans, cognitive behavioral therapists balance basing the measurement of progress on observable behavior without being excessively rigid because what is "appropriate" in one interpersonal interaction might be very different in another. Shane's therapist resolved

FIGURE 1.7

Problem Area	Manifestations of Problem Area	Indicators of Progress	Therapeutic Intervention
Problem Area #1 Problems in romantic relationships	1. Limited social skills 2. Difficulty accurately inferring social cues 3. Inaccurate expectations for relationships	1. Remain in conversation until it naturally comes to a close. 2. Verify interpersonal assumptions before acting on them. 3. Initiate an appropriate number of connections with potential romantic partners. 4. Tolerate infrequent contact with potential romantic partners at the beginning of a relationship.	1. Social skills training 2. Social problem solving 3. Cognitive restructuring

Portion of completed treatment plan.

to work with him to develop the cognitive and behavioral flexibility to make these determinations on a case-by-case basis, evaluating success on the basis of the frequency with which women remained in the conversation with him and agreed to go on a date with him.

Finally, treatment plans incorporate the specific therapeutic interventions that are expected to be useful in helping clients address problem areas. For example, Shane's therapist recognized that social skills training and social problem solving (described in Chapter 3 of this volume) would be useful in helping him to develop social skills and arrive upon more adaptive solutions to ambiguous interpersonal dilemmas that he faced. Moreover, she suspected that cognitive restructuring (described in Chapters 4 and 5 of this volume) would help him recognize unhelpful thinking that prompted him to behave in maladaptive ways during interactions with potential romantic partners, as well as rigid rules and assumptions that he held about ways that potential romantic partners "should" respond to him.

Treatment plans are always developed in collaboration with the client. If the client does not wish to work on an issue, even if the therapist views that issue as a problem in the client's life, then it generally is not included on the treatment plan (however, the therapist can certainly reintroduce the issue at another time to determine whether the client now sees a need to work on the issue in therapy). The exception to this is if the client is at moderate to high risk for suicidal behavior, in which case the reduction in risk for suicidal behavior would assume focus as the primary goal of treatment (Wenzel et al., 2009).

There are many rules of thumb for the prioritization of problem areas that are not related to suicidal behavior. Sometimes, the therapist may simply ask the client which problem they think would be the best place to start. At other times, therapist may suggest beginning with the problem that is causing the greatest amount of life interference or is the longest standing. Or, if one problem area seems more manageable than other problem areas, it may seem sensible to address that problem area first. This latter choice of starting with the easier problem allows the client the opportunity to acquire valuable cognitive and behavioral tools that can be applied to a host of problem areas. It also allows clients to develop a sense of self-efficacy, such that they develop the belief that they can indeed make positive changes in their lives. Such success not only instills hope, but it also enhances clients' perceptions of the quality of the therapeutic alliance (DeRubeis, Brotman, & Gibbons, 2005; DeRubeis & Feeley, 1990; Feeley, DeRubeis, & Gelfand, 1999; Webb et al., 2011), which is in turn associated with positive outcomes in psychotherapy (Martin, Garske, & Davis, 2000).

It is important to be cognizant to use treatment plans *throughout* the course of CBT. It is not uncommon for therapists to develop well-thought-out treatment plans only to leave them languishing in clients' charts for the duration of treatment. We recommend that cognitive behavioral therapists review treatment goals periodically throughout the course of treatment. *Periodically* has different meanings for different clients. For a client with a mild case of a single mental health disorder, the treatment plan might be reviewed every three sessions because the course of treatment would expected to be time-limited. Other clients, such as those with personality disorders or those with significant comorbidity, might be in treatment for a year or more, so it would be appropriate to review the treatment plan less frequently (e.g., every 2 months). During the review of the treatment plan, cognitive behavioral therapists assess the degree to which clients have resolved the problem area and whether any additional problem areas need to be added to the treatment plan. In Chapter 6, we describe indicators that signify when clients can move into the late phase of therapy, which is focused on relapse prevention and the ending of regular sessions.

Conclusion

Psychological assessment is an essential part of the work of cognitive behavioral therapists. It establishes diagnoses of mental health disorders; identifies the etiological, maintenance, and exacerbation factors of mental health problems; and supplies information about modifiable psychological factors that could be targets of treatment. There are multiple modalities for assessment, including clinical interviews, self-report inventories, self-monitoring, behavioral observation, and collateral information. Mental health professionals evaluate each of these pieces of information on their own (often compared with normative data to judge the degree to which the data are normal or abnormal), and integrate these pieces with one another to arrive at a comprehensive case conceptualization, including diagnosis, of the client's clinical presentations.

Cognitive behavioral therapists apply the information derived from the psychological assessment to the case conceptualization. The case conceptualization allows the therapist to apply cognitive behavioral theory to the individual client, depicting the cognitive and behavioral factors that explain the client's clinical presentation. It helps the therapist to make sense of unexpected events in treatment, such as crises or ruptures in the therapeutic relationship. It also points to modifiable psychological factors that can serve as the targets of treatment.

Assessment does not end after the first few sessions with a client. Rather, it continues across the course of therapy, as the cognitive behavioral therapist obtains mood checks at the beginning of each session and periodically reviews the treatment plan. If it is determined collaboratively with the client that progress toward resolving problem areas is not going as hoped or if new issues arise, then the treatment plan is revised. Thus, cognitive behavioral therapists approach their clinical work with equal foci on assessment and psychotherapy, all the while prioritizing the therapeutic alliance and collaboration with the client.

The therapeutic interventions delivered in the course of treatment follow logically from the case conceptualization. The subsequent chapters of this volume describe many standard cognitive and behavioral techniques that are commonly delivered for clinical presentations such as depression and anxiety. The field is ever advancing, and new treatment frameworks and techniques are continually being developed. Therapists often wonder if they are "still doing CBT" if they integrate a technique from a therapeutic approach that they deem to be different from CBT. In point of fact, expert cognitive therapists have long advocated for the flexible delivery of CBT (Alford & Beck, 1997b) within the context of a coherent theory of psychopathology (i.e., the case conceptualization).

Thus, cognitive behavioral therapists integrate many techniques from other psychotherapies (e.g., empty chair from Gestalt therapy, cognitive defusion acceptance and commitment therapy) in the service of meaning treatment goals that emerge from the case conceptualization (Alford & Beck, 1997a; Petrik, Kazantzis, & Hofmann, 2013). Moreover, as mentioned in the Introduction to this volume, cognitive behavioral therapists are increasingly adopting a transdiagnostic approach to the conceptualization and treatment of psychopathology, meaning that they are placing particular emphasis on the psychological underpinnings of and processes associated with cognitive, emotional, and behavioral patterns that cut across single diagnoses of mental health disorders (Barlow et al., 2011). Although the subsequent chapters describe a fairly standard application of CBT techniques, readers are encouraged to think flexibly and creatively about alternative strategies that would achieve similar goals.

Session Structure and Behavioral Strategies

2

ognitive behavioral therapy (CBT) is an active, problem-focused approach to treatment. Not only are specific goals set for the overall course of treatment, but a focus for each session is also decided on collaboratively by the therapist and client at the beginning of each session. The aim is for clients to leave each session with something new that is expected to make a difference in their lives in between sessions, whether that something new is a skill or a tool, a solution to a problem, or a new way to view their life circumstances. To accomplish these aims, cognitive behavioral therapists structure the treatment session to ensure that their therapeutic work is focused.

Behavioral strategies are some of the most direct and straightforward methods used by cognitive behavioral therapists because they are inherently active and problem focused. In some instances, when clients do something differently, they experience fairly immediate changes in their lives. Moreover, the successful implementation of behavioral changes can

http://dx.doi.org/10.1037/14936-003
Cognitive Behavioral Therapy Techniques and Strategies, by A. Wenzel, K. S. Dobson, and P. A. Hays

serve as an important learning experience for clients because it instills hope that their lives can be different, and it helps clients to develop a sense of self-efficacy. These realizations can, in turn, increase their commitment to further change and to practice with successful strategies and techniques offer.

In this chapter, we describe the typical session structure that is used by cognitive behavioral therapists. We demonstrate the manner in which they set the stage for the implementation of strategic cognitive and behavioral interventions, as well as the manner in which they provide therapeutic benefits in and of themselves. In addition, we describe a sampling of standard behavioral strategies used by cognitive behavioral therapists for many common clinical presentations.

Session Structure

Cognitive behavioral therapists typically implement session structure to ensure that (a) their work with clients is focused and efficient, (b) progress is being made toward treatment goals, and (c) seemingly disparate problems are addressed in a coherent and organized manner. When clients first present for treatment, they are often overwhelmed and express that they do not know where to turn or what to do next. Session structure can provide a template to disentangle, understand, and then implement solutions to these problems.

The components of typical CBT session structure are as follows: (a) brief mood check; (b) bridge from the previous session; (c) agenda setting; (d) discussion of the accepted agenda items, including review of previous homework; (e) development of new homework; and (f) final summary and feedback. Each of these session structure components is discussed in this section. However, cognitive behavioral therapists need not be limited to these specific components. Some clients, for example, repeatedly present for session in an agitated state, and it can be helpful to open the session with a breathing, relaxation, or other grounding exercise before proceeding. Other clients, especially children and adolescents, may arrive at therapy accompanied by a family member, and it could be helpful to reserve a brief time at the outset of the session for the family member to provide observations of the client's behavior in between sessions or, at the end of the session, to update the family member on next steps intended in therapy. On rare occasions, some clients find one or more aspects of session structure aversive or inconsistent with their personal style, which is important feedback for the therapist and suggests the need to adjust the manner in which sessions are conducted.

CBT session structure need not be implemented in a rigid or mechanistic manner. Many novice cognitive behavioral therapists mistakenly believe that these components are like items on a list that should be checked off (and, at times, will even bring a homemade checklist into session to prompt themselves to cover each session structure component). On the contrary, cognitive behavioral therapists implement session structure in a fluid, conversational manner, balancing attention to structure with genuine here-and-now interaction with the client.

BRIEF MOOD CHECK

Cognitive behavioral therapists typically obtain mood ratings from their clients so that they can understand the degree to which their mental health symptoms are changing as a result of therapy. As highlighted in the previous chapter, the *brief mood check* is one manner in which assessment continues throughout the course of therapy.

There is no singular or "right" way to conduct the brief mood check. Some cognitive behavioral therapists ask their clients to complete brief self-report inventories of various symptoms associated with mood disturbance, such as the Beck Depression Inventory—II (BDI–II; A. T. Beck, Steer, & Brown, 1996). Other cognitive behavioral therapists ask their clients to make ratings on a Likert-type scale. For example, clients could be asked to rate their depression in the time between sessions on a 0-to-10 scale, such that 0 would signify the *absence of depression*, and 10 would signify the *most severe depression* one could imagine experiencing. If the client prefers, a percentage rating could replace a 0-to-10 rating scale (e.g., 10%, 90%). Clients can complete self-report inventories, make Likert-type mood ratings, or give percentage ratings for other key aspects of their clinical presentations, such as anxiety, sleep disturbance, marital dissatisfaction, or compulsive behavior. Therapists who work with clients who are at risk for suicidal behavior might conduct an abbreviated suicide risk assessment, focusing on the frequency, severity, and duration of suicidal ideation, suicidal intent, suicidal gestures, and hopelessness. Therapists who work with clients with substance use problems might obtain an estimate of the frequency and quantity of alcohol or drug use. We recommend that the data collected in the brief mood check be quantitative, rather than qualitative (e.g., "How is your mood?") to facilitate comparison across sessions. In fact, many clients find it valuable to graph the mood ratings obtained across the course of several sessions so that they can attain a sense of their progress in treatment.

The brief mood check is usually quite straightforward and consists of only a few exchanges before moving on. The therapist might ask, "On our scale of 0 to 10, with 0 being the absence of depression and 10 being the most depression you can imagine experiencing, what rating would characterize the depression experienced in the time between sessions?" The client would supply a rating, and, in response, the therapist would then make a supportive comment that expresses a genuine sense of pleasure if the rating has decreased, or a genuine sense of empathy if the rating is high or increased. If the mood rating changes noticeably, the therapist might ask to what the client attributes this change. If the mood rating has decreased, it is helpful to know whether the client believes that his or her cognitive behavioral tools have been helpful. If the mood rating has increased, it is helpful to know whether the client believes that his or her cognitive behavioral tools have been unhelpful or whether there is a new issue that should be addressed in therapy.

The brief mood check may be less straightforward if the client launches into excessive detail about an upsetting event that occurred between sessions, or if the client resists supplying the ratings. In the former instance, cognitive behavioral therapists typically express empathy and invite the client to make that issue the highest priority on the session's agenda. In the latter instance, cognitive behavioral therapists listen carefully to their client's concern, confirm that their client understands the rationale for making the rating, and invite collaboration to decide whether the format for the mood check is the problem and whether to conduct the session differently.

BRIDGE FROM PREVIOUS SESSION

The bridge from the previous session provides an opportunity for clients to recall their work from the previous session and express the degree to which it was helpful and whether anything did not sit well with them. The bridge often sets the stage for the work to be done in the current session, addressing the questions "Where have we been recently?" and "What is the next step that can be taken to get to where we are going?"

From our perspective, simply asking clients whether the previous session was helpful does not yield much information that is useful for shaping the current session because most clients respond affirmatively. Instead, cognitive behavioral therapists ask questions such as, "What did you take away from the previous session?" "What from the previous session ended up making a difference in the time between sessions?" or "Did the work you did in between sessions provide any new information for us or for today's session?" These more detailed questions allow clients the opportunity to elaborate on their experience and what they found helpful. Moreover, questions of this nature provide a forum for clients to put their own words to the cognitive behavioral principles that their therapists are hoping to instill in them, which is important for the consolidation of learning. In addition, as J. S. Beck (2011) recommended, we encourage cognitive behavioral therapists to ask their clients whether they had a negative reaction to anything that occurred in the previous session or to anything that the therapist said in the previous session. This communicates to clients that their opinions are important and that honest feedback will be taken seriously.

AGENDA

The agenda consists of the topics the therapist and client agreed to cover in the current session. The agenda is typically developed collaboratively at the beginning of the session, during or after the brief mood check and the bridge from the previous session. Although there is no hard-and-fast rule for the number of items to include on the agenda, most agendas include between one and three items. Generally, it is better to fully discuss a smaller number of items than to try to cram too much into a session and cover items poorly.

Agenda items should be specific; vague agenda items often lead to unfocused, general discussion that are not associated with a clear goal. Thus, if a client is asked for an agenda topic and responds with a something like "my relationship with my spouse," the therapist might ask if there is a specific aspect of the spousal relationship that they should address. Alternatively, the therapist might ask what the client hopes to achieve by addressing that topic.

There will be occasions when a cognitive behavioral therapist asks a client what he or she would like to address in session, and the client responds, "I don't know." This type of response usually reflects incomplete socialization of the client into CBT structure and process. Thus, we recommend that cognitive behavioral therapists educate their clients early in the process of therapy about the purpose of the agenda and the role of both the therapist and client in setting the agenda. If a client continues to indicate that he or she does not know what to put on the agenda, then this issue, itself, can be a topic for the agenda. For example, such discussion might elucidate a larger pattern of avoidance behavior that could assume a central focus in treatment.

It is fairly common for clients to jump into unfocused discussion before setting the agenda. Often, these clients need to be socialized into the process of simply identifying and naming the problem. If the therapist does not intervene gently and redirect the client, then the therapist runs the risk of reinforcing the same disorganized way the client approaches his or her life problems outside of session. When therapists find themselves in this situation, they can take the first opportunity to respond, expressing empathy as well as calling attention to the agenda by saying something such as, "It sounds like this is an important problem that has been on your mind this week. Should we make sure to make this the main focus of today's session?" In addition, before moving onto discussion of that issue, therapists can say something such as, "OK, we will focus on this. Before we jump in, however, I'd like to make sure that we cover everything that is important to cover. Is there anything else we should be sure to reserve time to address today?"

Novice therapists can become overwhelmed with the components of session structure discussed thus far or put pressure on themselves to make sure that they "cover" everything. The following dialogue with Beth, one of the clients introduced in Chapter 1, demonstrates the way in which these components come together in a fluid manner at the beginning of a CBT session.

Therapist: Beth, come in. It's good to see you here today.

Beth: [looking down at her hands] Thanks. It's been a tough week.

Therapist: I'm sorry to hear that it's been a tough week. I'm wondering if that's affected your mood? [Beth nods.] On our depression scale, with *0* being the absence of depression and *10* being the most depression that you can imagine experiencing, what rating characterizes your mood over the past week?

Beth: [tearful] I think it's gotten to a *10*. The kids are out of control. I just can't seem to do anything right this week.

Therapist: [displaying a great deal of empathy with her facial expression] You're right, that does sound rough. We've been talking about how to handle crises that arise in your classroom. Is it fair to say that we should continue that discussion today?

Beth: Oh, yes, definitely.

Therapist: Is there one particular crisis that we should discuss to be as focused as possible?

Beth: There were two that happened, actually. One on Monday and another one this morning. I'm really shaken up by them. I'm just really afraid that I'm going to lose my job, and then what? I'll have no money, no way to live. [escalating] Gosh, I'm such a loser. Why did I even take this job? [puts head in hands, leaving an opening for the therapist to intervene and finish setting the agenda]

Therapist: [leans forward] I have an idea. Let's talk about both incidents. Perhaps what we can do is keep an eye for common themes that run across both of them so that we can identify some approaches for dealing with similar crises in the future. How does that sound?

Beth: [nods] Yes, that would be good.

Therapist: I also noticed, as you were talking, that you have some concerns about the consequences if you do not handle these incidents effectively. These have also come up in our discussions in previous visits. Is it OK with you if we leave some time toward the end to focus on these concerns as well?

Beth: Definitely. They consume me, really. I think the anxiety associated with my fear of getting fired is almost worse than having to deal with the kids in the moment when they are out of control.

Therapist: Ah, you mentioned anxiety. We've also been tracking your anxiety levels in addition to your depression levels, using the same scale. Where would you put your anxiety since the last time I saw you?

Beth: Same as my depression—a *10*. Sometimes they are different, but today both are sky high. It's been a horrible week.

Therapist: Yes, it does sound like this week, in particular, has been one of the worst for you. Throughout our conversation, we'll be sure to identify points at which the depression and anxiety are triggered and ways to cope with that.

Beth: Great. I really need some tools to help me through this time.

Therapist: Before we get started, I'd just like to check in with you regarding last week's visit. I'm wondering what you took away from that visit, and especially whether anything that we covered last time was useful in dealing with the two incidents that were upsetting to you this week.

Beth: Um [thinking] . . . I'm not sure. I know we've been working on how to cope with the way I think about my life. But I wasn't sure how to apply it in these situations.

Therapist: Would it be OK if, as we discuss the two incidents as well as your concerns about their consequences, we applied the skills that we've been developing?

Beth: [breathing a sigh of relief] I'd really like that. I think I need a lot of practice.

Therapist: [smiling] Well, this is what I'm here for. Let's take a look at the first incident that threw you for a loop.

Notice in this dialogue that the cognitive behavioral therapist addressed the three aspects of session structure as appropriate, rather than according to a prescribed order. When Beth indicated that it had been a tough week, her therapist expressed empathy and support before conducting the brief mood check. When Beth mentioned problems at her job, the therapist linked back to the topic of discussion in previous sessions and moved toward an agenda item when he asked Beth if they should continue to focus on problematic incidents in her classroom. However, the therapist also asked Beth to identify a specific incident so that they would have a clear focus of their discussion. When Beth began to escalate as she identified two incidents and expressed concern about their implications for her job, her therapist intervened to prevent further escalation and also propose a plan for the session, which solidified the agenda and communicated hope that they could make headway in addressing Beth's problems. Beth's therapist noted her catastrophic thinking as an additional but related problem to her difficulty handling crises, and he proposed that they also devote some time to applying cognitive behavioral skills for addressing them. As the conversation progressed, Beth's therapist obtained a second mood rating—that for anxiety—in response to Beth's observation that she was quite anxious. Finally, Beth's therapist asked Beth for feedback regarding what she learned from the previous session and her ability to apply the cognitive behavioral work that they had done together so far in the course of treatment (i.e., bridge from previous session). Because Beth expressed some difficulty in applying the work done in session to incidents that occurred in her life, her therapist gave her assurance that as the discussion of agenda items progressed, they would reinforce and practice the skills she had acquired to date.

DISCUSSION OF AGENDA ITEMS

A logical outgrowth of setting the agenda is to begin discussion of agenda items. The client often chooses the first agenda items to discuss, and it is typically the most distressing current situation or issue that he or she faces. However, if the therapist has a strong opinion about the first item to be covered, he or she can ask the client's permission to address that concern first.

During discussion of agenda items, cognitive behavioral therapists make *periodic summaries* of the main themes that their client has expressed to ensure that they have an accurate understanding and that they communicate their careful listening to the client. Cognitive behavioral therapists often ask clients to summarize their understanding of one agenda item as they begin to move to the next to consolidate their learning and reinforce the conclusion that was drawn from the conversation.

Some therapists believe that the concept of the agenda is limiting and that it stifles spontaneous discussion or boxes a therapist into a prescribed amount of time for each predetermined topic. It is important to note, however, that the agenda can change as the session progresses. When cognitive behavioral therapists notice that discussion of one agenda is taking the majority of session time, leaving little time for other agenda items, they say something to their client such as, "I'm noticing that we've spent the bulk of our time on this topic, and we had two other topics that we wanted to cover. In light of our agenda and the remaining time, how best should we focus our attention?" In response to this question, some clients choose to shift foci, whereas other clients opt to continue discussion on the topic at hand and "table" the other topics until the next session. Similarly, when cognitive behavioral therapists notice that a new topic has arisen, they say something to their client such as, "This sounds like an important topic that we didn't anticipate covering today. Should we use the rest of our time addressing this issue, or would you like me to write it down and save it for another session?" The key issue is that cognitive behavioral therapists are mindful of the agenda and make adjustments to it, with clients, as needed, rather than abandoning it entirely if the session takes a different direction than anticipated. Responding to shifts in the agenda in a flexible manner provides another opportunity for cognitive behavioral therapists to model, in session, an organized approach to addressing multiple life problems.

HOMEWORK

Homework is a term that refers to work that clients do between therapy sessions to translate the in session work to problems that they experience in their daily lives. Homework is central to CBT; cognitive behavioral therapists view homework as essential for new learning to occur. A growing body of research suggests that homework is strongly associated with outcome. For example, in a meta-analysis of 46 studies, Kazantzis, Whittington, and Dattilio (2010) determined that 62% of clients improve when they participate in therapy with homework, relative to 38% of patients who participate in therapy without homework. Client adherence to homework assignments is associated with reduced depression (e.g., Cowan et al., 2008; Rees, McEvoy, & Nathan, 2005), reduced anxiety (Rees et al., 2005; Westra, Dozois, & Marcus, 2007), reduced substance use (Gonzalez, Schmitz, & DeLaunne, 2006), improved social support (Cowan et al., 2008), and improved quality of life (Rees et al., 2005). Most clients view homework favorably and see it as key to their progress in treatment (Fehm & Mrose, 2008).

Homework is integrated into CBT session structure in two ways. Cognitive behavioral therapists work collaboratively with their clients to develop homework that clients can implement in between sessions, with the idea that the homework will either yield important information about the client's life problems, or that the exercise will itself make a meaningful difference in the client's life. Notice that we are using the term homework *exercise* rather than homework *assignment*. Some clients say that the term *assignment* evokes memories from school in which the teacher was the authority and unilaterally determined the content of the homework. In contrast, the content of CBT homework is determined equally by the therapist and the client, with the client having the ultimate say in what and how much he or she will do for homework. It is also important for clients to understand and buy into the rationale for homework, which could increase their commitment to following through with it. We often tell our clients that they spend much more time outside of their session than in session with their therapist and that homework is one way to bridge the work that they have done in session to their daily lives.

Homework is a highly flexible tool. This book includes many CBT strategies, including behavioral activation and exposure (this chapter), problem solving (Chapter 3), acceptance (Chapter 3), cognitive restructuring of automatic thoughts (Chapter 4), cognitive restructuring of beliefs (Chapter 5), and relapse prevention (Chapter 6). There are specific techniques associated with each of these strategies, and many of these techniques can be translated into homework exercises to be completed in between sessions. However, any task that the client believes would be helpful can serve as homework. For example, a client with an alcohol use disorder might commit to going to an Alcoholics Anonymous meeting. A client with insomnia might maintain a sleep log, keeping track of his sleep and variables that might affect it. A client with obesity might decide to cook her meals during the week, rather than eat out at restaurants.

Although we discuss the development of homework near the close of this section on session structure, it is important to acknowledge that homework need not be developed at the end of the session. In fact, homework is often best when it grows during the discussion of the agenda items. If a homework exercise naturally follows from discussion of the first agenda item, then the therapist and client can develop that before moving on to other agenda items. Leaving the development of homework for the last minutes of the session can be problematic because there might not be enough time to develop it thoroughly or in a way that the client truly understands and buys into. Exhibit 2.1 displays other tips for maximizing the effectiveness of homework.

The second way that homework is integrated into CBT sessions is in its review, often early in the next session. Homework review is essential; ignoring homework communicates that it is unimportant. Moreover, it is important to validate the hard work that the client did in between sessions. Even if the client did not complete the homework, it is important to understand the obstacles that interfered with homework

---

EXHIBIT 2.1

Maximizing the Effectiveness of Homework

- Ask clients to state in their own words why they think homework will be useful to increase motivation and ownership.
- Begin or practice the homework exercise in session.
- Ask clients to indicate the likelihood of completing the homework exercise in between sessions and modify it if the likelihood is less than 90%.
- Identify obstacles to completing the homework and ways to overcome those obstacles.
- Ask clients to identify when they expect to complete the homework.
- Ask clients to identify where they will keep the homework if it requires handwriting.
- Develop a backup plan in case homework does not go as anticipated.

---

completion and identify ways to make homework more helpful and effective in the future. Homework review can be done in many ways. Some cognitive behavioral therapists review homework before they set an agenda for the session if discussion of homework is brief; other cognitive behavioral therapists suggest that they make it an agenda item for lengthier discussion. At times, the homework exercise itself contains references to important events that occurred in the time between sessions (e.g., a thought record; see Chapter 4), so the therapist and client can structure the session around those events, simultaneously discussing what happened and reviewing the homework.

Homework review is more than simply praising the client for completing the exercise. Cognitive behavioral therapists demonstrate a great deal of curiosity about the client's experience with the homework, prompting clients to reflect on conclusions they drew from the homework, ways they homework made a difference in their lives, and ways in which they will carry forward the "lessons learned" from homework to build on their progress. This is another opportunity to promote the consolidation of clients' learning and allow them to take ownership over the new learning that has occurred.

Another key aspect of the review of homework is to identify both exercises that went well and those with which the client struggled. Positive homework experiences should be acknowledged, and the therapist can look for an opportunity to build on this success. Furthermore, some longer term therapy goals may require a progressive set of steps that take place across weeks or even months of treatment. It is important that the therapist tracks these issues along with the client to monitor progress and provide corrective action when needed. Moreover, negative experiences with homework are just as important to discuss in session. Such a discussion may suggest the need for skills building, addressing the client's persistence in the face of obstacles, or a reconsideration of environmental or interpersonal variables that may work against change. For more elaboration on these strategies for the effective integration of homework into CBT, as well as for discussion of additional strategies, Kazantzis, Deane, Ronan, and L'Abate (2005) is an excellent resource.

FINAL SUMMARY AND FEEDBACK

At the close of the session, the therapist and client summarize their work and the main conclusions that emerged from that work. Cognitive behavioral therapists ask questions similar to those asked during the bridge from the previous session, such as, "What do you take from today's session?" or "What about today's session do you expect to make the biggest difference in your life?" At times, clients make keen observations about the final agenda item but do not earlier agenda items (i.e., a recency effect). In these instances, cognitive behavioral therapists acknowledge the learning that occurred earlier in the session. In addition to asking questions designed to consolidate learning and translate the client's knowledge to his or her life outside of session, cognitive behavioral therapists obtain feedback to ensure that the client was satisfied with the session and that nothing occurred to adversely affect the therapeutic relationship. For example, the therapist might ask something such as, "Was there anything that I said or did that bothered you or that you thought I got wrong?"

Behavioral Strategies

As their name suggests, behavioral strategies intervene at the level of a client's behavior. In other words, therapists use behavioral strategies to help clients to do things differently in their lives. Doing things differently could mean that clients increase their engagement in activities that they find rewarding, overcome avoidance of activities that seem overwhelming, or engage in healthy behaviors to improve their self-care. It is important to recognize that the positive impact of behavioral strategies is not limited to an impact on clients' behavior; in fact, successful implementation of behavioral strategies often facilitates cognitive change. For example, clients who benefit from behavioral strategies often develop a sense of hope and optimism that their lives can be different, which further increases their commitment to their behavioral efforts. Other clients realize that the aversive outcomes that they expected to occur in fact do not. Still other clients learn that they have the strength and resources to solve problems in their lives. In this section, we consider two behavioral strategies used frequently by cognitive behavioral therapists—behavioral activation and exposure.

BEHAVIORAL ACTIVATION

According to behavioral theories of depression (e.g., Lewinsohn, 1974), depression can be explained, in part, by the failure to engage in activities that provide a sense of reward or reinforcement. When people are depressed, it makes sense that they decrease their activity level because of low energy and motivation. However, activity decrease does not facilitate recovery; instead, it increases depression because it deprives individuals of the opportunity to engage in meaningful activities. Thus, depressed clients often fall into a vicious cycle—the more depressed they feel, the more they forgo opportunities to engage in activities that give them a sense of joy or pleasure, and the more they forgo the activities that give them a sense of joy or pleasure, the less response-contingent reward they obtain and so the more depressed they feel.

Behavioral activation involves a set of techniques that help clients reengage in activities that give a sense of satisfaction, accomplishment, and pleasure. In other words, behavioral activation is designed to increase the frequency with which clients engage in activities that provide reward to break the vicious cycle of depression. Behavioral activation is both a stand-alone treatment for depression (Martell, Dimidjian, & Herman-Dunn, 2010) and an important component of cognitive behavioral treatment packages for depression (J. S. Beck, 2011).

Two important techniques that facilitate behavioral activation are activity monitoring and activity scheduling. Clients who engage in *activity monitoring* track the manner in which they spend their time in between sessions on an activity log. The idea behind activity monitoring is the therapist and client can collect baseline data that capture the manner in which the client is spending his or her time, as well as the amount of accomplishment and pleasure associated with activities (rated on a 0-to-10 scale; 0 = *no accomplishment or pleasure*, 10 = *the most accomplishment or pleasure one could imagine*). These baseline data are critically examined at the time of the subsequent session, and space is given to the client to draw conclusions about the ways the activities in which he or she engages might be exacerbating depression, rather than helping it. It is expected that clients' depression ratings would be higher on days in which they are particularly disengaged and getting little reward.

The next logical step after activity monitoring is *activity scheduling*, such that the client plans to engage in activities that are expected to yield a greater sense of reward at key times during the week. Clients can record the activities they plan with a new activity log, and in between sessions, they can record the activities in which they engage and make ratings of accomplishment, pleasure, and overall depression, as well as indicate the planned activities with which they follow through. It is expected that their overall depression ratings made at the end of the day will be lower after they have implemented the activities that they have scheduled, and also lower relative to when they simply monitored their activities, because they are getting a greater sense of pleasure and accomplishment in their lives.

It has been suggested that behavioral activation is useful with severely depressed clients in particular, because increased engagement has a relatively immediate antidepressant effect, and it could give these clients the boost that they need to engage in other strategies that CBT has to offer, such as cognitive restructuring (e.g., A. T. Beck, Rush, Shaw, & Emery, 1979). Thus, behavioral activation is often implemented in the early and early-middle phases of treatment. At times, however, the very act of recording activities every hour of the day can be overwhelming for depressed clients. Cognitive behavioral therapists modify activity monitoring to their clients' level of functioning. For example, clients can divide the day into a few chunks and write down what happened in those chunks. They can also record activities for only a few days in between sessions, such as 2 weekdays and 1 weekend day. They can make use of time sampling, such that they program their smartphones to signal reminders to record activities at various intervals. Or they can work with their therapist to develop a more focused checklist of activities associated with pleasure and a sense of accomplishment, so that they simply have to indicate with a check mark when they engage in those activities (Martell et al., 2010; Wenzel, 2013).

Activity scheduling need not proceed in a rigid manner, such that clients are locked into in a particular activity on a particular day and at a particular hour. In fact, many clients prefer to target activities on a particular day or part of the day (e.g., "Tuesday morning," "Friday night"), rather than at a particular hour. It is also important to have backup plans because it is easy for depressed clients to become discouraged and abandon their activity schedule if they miss an activity. The backup plan might be a different day in which to engage in the activity (e.g., going to the gym on a Wednesday if the client did not make it there on a Tuesday), or it might be a different activity in which to engage at the same time if an obstacle is encountered (e.g., go to a yoga class indoors if a storm prevents the client from walking outdoors).

The following extended dialogue illustrates the manner in which behavioral activation was implemented with Shane, one of the clients introduced in Chapter 1. Shane described a pattern of social isolation, such that he comes home to his apartment after work and on weekends and remains alone much of the time. He remarked that as he is getting older, his friends are increasingly involved with their romantic partners and starting families, and he does not want to be a burden to them. He also mentioned that he is quite bored at home, and with nothing to do he drinks alcohol, which increases his focus on his unhappiness and, increases the frequency, severity, and duration of his suicidal ideation. His therapist reasoned that behavioral activation would help him to engage in activities that would both reduce his self-focused attention and increase his joy and reasons for living. However, given Shane's guardedness as well as his expectation that there would be a "quick cure" for his depression, his therapist experienced some challenges when implementing these techniques with him.

Shane: I don't know. I really don't know if this is going to help. It seems like a lot of work for very little result.

Therapist: I can appreciate that it seems like work, Shane. Can you tell me why I suggested that you monitor how you spend your time between sessions?

Shane: I guess so we can see if I'm being productive.

Therapist: Well, from my point of view, I'm less concerned about you being productive per se, particularly in your free time outside of work. I'm more concerned about you doing things that give you pleasure and satisfaction, regardless of whether they're productive. My hunch here is that you have a lot of time in which you're not getting a lot of pleasure and satisfaction, and I think that is making your depression worse. So if we can identify more specifically where this is occurring, then we might be able to work in some more meaningful activities and begin to chip away at your depression. What do you think—do you buy this rationale?

Shane: Well, yeah, in theory, who doesn't want to do things that they enjoy? The problem, though, is that I really don't know what brings me joy anymore. Even drinking. I don't really enjoy it. It just passes time and numbs me out, makes me not think about things.

Therapist: [staying with behavioral activation and choosing not to question Shane's view that drinking makes him not think about his life] You're not the first person who's said to me that they don't know what they would do to get enjoyment or pleasure. I can help with that. What we need to do, though, is figure out where to start. And that's where this monitoring comes in.

Shane: [looking at the activity log] Every hour of the day? No way, I don't think I can commit to that.

Therapist: I understand and agree with you—it *is* a lot to commit to. What if we scaled it down?

Shane: What, you mean like just writing down how I spend my time in the evenings?

Therapist: Sure, that's one way to scale down if you think that would be best for you.

Shane: Yeah, I think that is much more doable. I really do the same thing all the time at work. Evenings are when I feel the worst.

Therapist: So what if we were to make a revised activity log focusing on the hours of 5 p.m. through 11 p.m. when you go to bed? And you can rate how depressed you feel right before bed?

Shane: Yeah, let's do that.

Shane and his therapist proceeded to sit side by side at her computer and create a customized activity log that he would use to record his activities in the evenings, as well as his depression level when he went to bed. She asked him if he was willing to record any notable activities or events that occurred during the day, because she suspected that Shane overgeneralized when he said he did the same thing every day at work. Shane continued to express his opinion that he was not interested in doing this, however, and, in the spirit of collaboration, she did not push him. At the time of the subsequent session 3 days later, Shane indicated that he had completed the exercise and agreed to make review of homework the primary agenda item.

Therapist: It's terrific that you completed the activity monitoring. I know you were a bit ambivalent about it. What did you conclude from it?

Shane: That my life is totally depressing. See? I knew this would happen if I did this. It would just make me feel worse. It was a waste of time.

Therapist: I'm truly sorry to hear that you feel worse, but I'm hoping that, together, we can figure out a way to make good use of all of this information that you collected.

Shane: Yeah, whatever.

Therapist: Is it OK if I take a look and give you my impressions?

[Shane hands the therapist his activity log.]

Therapist: Hmmm, take a look at this. This is interesting to me. Yesterday, you were much less depressed than you were Monday and Tuesday evenings. Why do you think that is?

Shane: Oh, on Wednesday nights I go to my sister's house. We have always have spaghetti night.

Therapist: Do you think that had anything to do with the fact that your depression rating was 4 points lower than it was on Monday and Tuesday?

Shane: Well, yeah, that's a no-brainer. I love being with my sister. She's my favorite person in the whole world.

Therapist: [leaning forward] What does that tell you about things that you might do with your time in the evenings?

Shane: What, spend every single night with my sister? I think her boyfriend would get tired of that. Plus, she lives so far away—it's a real trek to get out there. And she has her own life, you know. I can't just impose on her. [escalating]

Therapist: [gently interrupting] I'm not necessarily thinking that you will spend every night with your sister. But I *am* wondering whether you might see her a little more frequently, say twice a week. And if there is someone else whom you get on well with, perhaps someone who lives a bit closer, whom you might be able to spend time with another day of the week.

Shane: I don't know, maybe. [pausing] Now that it's basketball season, maybe I can hang out with my sister and her boyfriend on a weekend day as well. We're all big basketball fans. We get in all kinds of tournament pools.

Therapist: [noticing Shane becoming more engaged and exhibiting more positive affect than he has in the past] That's exactly the kind of idea I was hoping that you would come up with. If you were to look forward to watching a basketball game with your sister and her boyfriend on the weekend, how would that affect your mood?

Shane: I think it would be good—definitely. Weekends really drag for me. But then I'm also miserable during the week. So this would give me something to look forward to.

Therapist: This coming weekend, when is there a game scheduled?

Shane: There are games pretty continuously all weekend long. But there are a couple of really good ones on Sunday.

Therapist: What would you think about making arrangements with your sister to watch one of those Sunday games?

Shane: Yeah, I think I'll do that.

Therapist: And just to plan for all possibilities, what will you do if your sister says she already has plans on Sunday?

Shane: Um, I can see if we can catch a game Saturday night. Or maybe I can go to my parents' house and watch a game with my dad.

Therapist: Ah, your dad. Do the two of you get along well?

Shane: Yeah, pretty well, I guess. A lot better now than when I was younger.

Therapist: And you share common interests, like basketball?

Shane: Sure. My family likes all kinds of sports.

Therapist: I think regarding your father as a backup plan, in case your sister already has plans, is a great idea. I'm also wondering if there is another time this week that you can visit with your dad.

Shane: Aw, I don't know, he's really busy. He owns his own business. So there's always a fire that he needs to put out. I don't want to bother him.

Therapist: So, in theory, you enjoy spending time with your dad, but things often come up that interfere with plans you might have with him?

Shane: Yeah.

Therapist: I wonder if we can put our heads together and figure out something that might work, whether it's a time in which your father is less likely to be interrupted or an activity that can withstand a bit of interruption.

Shane and his therapist used problem solving to entertain a number of possibilities, which helped Shane overcome his tendency to immediately judge and dismiss potential solutions to problems before he had fully considered ways to make them work. Shane agreed to keep another activity log, in which he summarized his evening and activities (and also weekend activities, given that the weekend would intervene between appointments) and rated his overall level of depression for the day. He agreed to work on two activities—watching a basketball game with his sister and her boyfriend and eating dinner at his parents' home on Monday evening (the evening in which his father's business closed early, thus decreasing the likelihood that they would be interrupted). At the time of his next therapy session, Shane's therapist invited discussion about the way in which the behavioral activation homework affected his mood.

> *Therapist:* What did you conclude from your homework this time?
>
> *Shane:* It was good to get out more. I drank less because I had to drive home, and I didn't have as many hopeless thoughts over the weekend.
>
> *Therapist:* So is it safe to say that homework put a bit of a dent in your depression?
>
> *Shane:* Yeah, sure, *this* weekend. But what about moving forward? [angrily] I can't just rely on my family every time I'm feeling depressed.
>
> *Therapist:* [demonstrating an openness to Shane's anger] You read my mind. What about moving forward? Would it be OK to talk some about ways to build on the momentum that you have created and ways to generalize your new learning to your life?
>
> *Shane:* Yeah, OK.

The goal of behavioral activation is to actively engage in activities that are expected to have an antidepressant effect, and although the concept is straightforward, its delivery can be quite complex. As was seen in the dialogue between Shane and his therapist, behavioral activation requires a sound therapeutic alliance so that clients experience the work done in session as collaborative and clients can take ownership over the changes they make in their lives. Moreover, it requires therapists to be aware of unhelpful automatic thoughts that decrease motivation or the likelihood that clients follow through with keeping their activity log or trying new activities. In addition, therapists use problem solving to help clients identify and overcome obstacles to implementing the activities that they expect will bring them joy and pleasure. They also work with their clients to identify ways to generalize the principles of behavioral activation beyond the short period of time between sessions so that these principles become a part of clients' behavioral repertoire and prevent relapse and recurrence. Thus, behavioral activation cannot be implemented in isolation from many of the other strategies discussed in this volume.

EXPOSURE

Exposure is defined as systematic and prolonged contact with a feared stimulus or situation (Abramowitz, Deacon, & Whiteside, 2011). Exposure is a key component in the cognitive behavioral treatment of anxiety, obsessive-compulsive-related, and trauma- and stressor-related disorders (Olatunji, Cisler, & Deacon, 2010). A central feature of the clinical presentation of these disorders is avoidant behavior, which maintains and exacerbates anxiety through negative reinforcement. That is, when a person with one of these disorders avoids a feared stimulus or situation, he or she is relived of emotional distress in the short term, which paradoxically increases the likelihood of avoidance in the future. Exposure helps clients to overcome avoidance and break free of that vicious cycle of anxiety and avoidance.

Exposure can be implemented in many forms. *In vivo exposure* occurs when clients have actual contact with a feared stimulus or situation. For example, a client with a spider phobia might work up to allowing a spider to crawl on her arm or a client with contamination fears associated with obsessive–compulsive disorder (OCD) might work up to touching doorknobs and toilet seats in public restrooms. *Imaginal exposure* occurs when clients imagine feared thoughts, images, and memories. It is used for clients who experience intrusive thoughts (e.g., thoughts that a patient views as profane or blasphemous), worries about hypothetical scenarios that might occur in the future (e.g., a family member getting in a car accident), or memories of a past trauma (e.g., being in combat). Imaginal exposure can also be used as a step along a hierarchy of fears for specific phobias, before real-life in vivo exposure. *Interoceptive exposure* occurs when clients with anxiety about uncomfortable bodily sensations intentionally engage in activities to bring on these sensations (e.g., spinning in a chair to experience a sense of dizziness). The specific type of exposure that therapists use will vary from client to client on the basis of the patient's cognitive case conceptualization. For example, a therapist who is treating a client with panic disorder who also has significant health anxiety might use in vivo exposure to help this client overcome avoidance of situations that she believes increase the likelihood of having a panic attack (e.g., elevators), imaginal exposure to face her fear of having a horrible disease like cancer, and interoceptive exposure to overcome avoidance of bringing on bodily sensations that she finds uncomfortable.

The CBT field is undergoing a bit of a paradigm shift regarding the mechanisms of action associated with exposure. For many years, exposure was thought to work by the mechanism of *habituation*, or the process through which the body and mind adapt to a novel stimulus. This theory suggests that a person who remains in prolonged contact with a feared stimulus or situation without avoiding or escaping will eventually notice a decrease in emotional distress. Thus, it was reasoned that exposure is successful when clients demonstrate less anxiety with each successive contact with a feared stimulus or situation, as well as when their peak anxiety during such contact decreases with successive trials (Foa & Kozak, 1986). Abramowitz et al. (2011) likened this process to getting accustomed to cold water in a swimming pool: The longer one stays in the water, the less cold it feels—not because the temperature of the water has changed, but because one's body has adapted.

However, data have accumulated that are contrary to these assumptions of habituation (Craske et al., 2008). Studies have demonstrated that within-session and between-session exposure was unrelated to outcome in exposure therapy for disorders such as OCD (Kozak, Foa, & Steketee, 1988), panic disorder (Riley et al., 1995), posttraumatic stress disorder (Pitman et al., 1996), and specific phobia (Lang & Craske, 2000). Moreover, it has been found that exposure is effective even when exposure trials are ended when the client still experiences a high level of anxiety, which, from a habituation standpoint, would be expected to reinforce avoidance and escape behavior (e.g., Emmelkamp & Mersch, 1982). In other words, the data suggest that habituation is not the primary mechanism that can account for the extinction of fear that is observed in the successful treatment of anxiety, obsessive-compulsive-related, and trauma- and stressor-related disorders.

An alternative theoretical framework to account for exposure's mechanism of action is *inhibitory learning.* According to Craske et al. (2008), inhibitory learning occurs when clients form new associations about the association between a feared stimulus or situation and an aversive outcome. Exposure offers clients many learning trials in which aversive outcomes do not occur despite contact with a feared stimulus or situation. This is regarded as an inhibitory association (vs. an excitatory association, when an aversive outcome indeed follows contact with a feared stimulus or situation). From the standpoint of inhibitory learning, fear reduction during and between exposure exercises is no longer regarded as essential for successful outcome in treatment. Thus, cognitive behavioral therapists who implement exposure from an inhibitory learning framework focus on fear tolerance rather than fear reduction.

The field is still evolving regarding guidelines for implementing exposure from an inhibitory learning perspective (Craske, Treanor, Conway, Zbozinek, & Vervliet, 2014). However, one aspect of exposure therapy that has not changed is the development of a fear hierarchy. A *fear hierarchy* is an ordered list of feared stimuli and situations, accompanied by ratings that capture the intensity of fear that is associated with each item. The items on the fear hierarchy serve as the stimuli or situations that will be encountered during exposure exercises. The ideal model is for clients to participate in an exposure exercise in session and then continue to practice exposure on their own for homework in between sessions (Wenzel, 2013).

Traditionally, exposure began with the item that was associated with the lowest level of fear, and once the client demonstrated habituation (i.e., reported lowered fear ratings during and between exposure exercises), the therapist would move on to the next item on the hierarchy. This sequence was followed in sequential order until clients attempted contact with the feared stimulus or situation that was associated with the highest fear rating. However, research by Lang and Craske (2000) suggests that outcome is actually enhanced when exposure is conducted with a random order to the hierarchy, as opposed to a sequential order. Craske et al. (2014) recommended that therapists begin with the lowest rated item on the hierarchy to guard against treatment refusal but then continue in random order.

When exposure proceeds from a habituation model, cognitive behavioral therapists collect periodic fear ratings during exposure exercises (using a 0 to 10 scale, such that 0 = *no fear* and 10 = *the most fear that one could imagine*) and asked their clients to track similar ratings on a recording form when they engaged in exposure in between sessions. When exposure is conducted from an inhibitory learning framework, fear ratings are greatly deemphasized, and instead, therapists focus on mismatching expectations to promote new learning (Craske et al., 2008). For example, clients might be asked how long they believe they can remain in contact with the feared stimulus or situation before something catastrophic happens, and they then participate in an exposure exercise that is longer than they predicted. To consolidate learning, clients are asked, before they participate in the exposure exercise, to indicate what they are worried would happen and the likelihood of that event's occurrence. After the exposure exercise, clients are invited to indicate whether the event actually occurred, how they know that, and what they learned (Craske et al., 2014).

Conclusion

CBT sessions assume some structure so that therapeutic work is as targeted and focused as possible. The main components of CBT session structure are the brief mood check, bridge from the previous session, development of a session agenda, discussion of agenda items (including homework review if it had not yet been done), development of new homework, and a final summary and feedback. However, session structure need not be implemented rigidly, and different cognitive behavioral therapists implement session structure in different ways. In fact, the same cognitive behavioral therapist might implement session structure in different ways with different clients. The key is that session structure is implemented in a smooth, conversational manner that enhances the therapeutic relationship and provides an organized framework for clients to address their life problems.

In our training and supervisory experience, we have observed that the quality of CBT sessions is positively associated with the degree to which session structure is implemented. Admittedly, there is a paucity of data to support this assertion. Nevertheless, when we train therapists to use session structure, some wonder whether the structure will somehow be off-putting or aversive for clients. In our experience, and to the contrary, many clients express much satisfaction with session structure because they realize that they struggle with disorganization and become easily overwhelmed and because the structure helps them to practice a different way to address their life problems. We encourage therapists who have concern about session structure (or any aspect of CBT) to treat those concerns of automatic thoughts to be tested on the basis of data, rather than worries or assumptions. When a therapist's evidence truly indicates that a patient is not responding as expected to session structure, the manner in which sessions are approached can be altered to take into account the client's preferences.

Behavioral activation refers to a strategic approach to help clients elicit response-contingent positive reinforcement from their environments or, in other words, to become more engaged in activities that are associated with a sense of pleasure, accomplishment, and meaning. The idea behind this strategy is for clients to recognize the association between depressed mood and lack of engagement in meaningful activities and, subsequently, to work those activities back into their routines. Research shows that behavioral activation is efficacious in the treatment of moderate to severe depression (Dimidjian et al., 2006). Thus, cognitive behavioral therapists who work with depressed clients should consider implementing behavioral activation in the early to middle phases of treatments so that clients can achieve an antidepressant effect that will activate them and put them in a position to address their life problems.

Exposure refers to systematic and prolonged contact with a feared stimulus or situation and is a central component of the cognitive behavioral treatment of anxiety, obsessive-compulsive-related, and trauma- or stressor-related disorders. At the time of the writing of this volume, the field is undergoing a substantial shift in the way in which cognitive behavioral therapists understand why exposure works and how best to implement it. According to the pioneering scholarship by Michelle

Craske and her colleagues, the effectiveness of exposure is maximized when cognitive behavioral therapists focus on creating opportunities for new learning and fear tolerance, rather than on fear reduction. We believe that this is an important development because anxiety is part of the normal human experience, and an important skill for all people to develop is a tolerance of risk, uncertainty, and adversity.

Behavioral activation and exposure are just two of many behavioral interventions that cognitive behavioral therapists can implement. Cognitive behavioral therapists also work with their patients to engage in behaviors to achieve optimal self-care (e.g., good sleep hygiene, diet, exercise), manage emotional distress (e.g., breathing, relaxation), and interact effectively with others (e.g., communication skills training). Regardless of the specific behavioral strategy implemented, it is expected that it will have a reciprocal relationship with cognition such that clients will begin to shift beliefs about their ineffectiveness and inadequacy as well as beliefs about the world being dangerous and uncontrollable.

Problem Solving | 3

P
roblems are a part of the normal human experience. Because
cognitive behavioral therapy (CBT) is an active, present-
focused approach to treatment, many clients focus their
attention on problems that they believe cause or exacerbate
their emotional distress. Problem solving, then, assumes a
central focus of treatment. According to Nezu, Nezu, and
D'Zurilla (2013), *problem-solving skills* are "the set of cognitive
behavioral activities by which a person attempts to discover
or develop effective solutions or ways of coping with real-life
problems" (p. 6). The idea that underpins problem-solving
interventions is that clients gain tools to understand, evaluate, and solve their problems, as well as overcome obstacles
that interfere with identifying or implementing solutions
to problems. As clients begin to solve their current problems, they also acquire and hone skills that can be applied to
solving future problems. It is also hoped that they develop
a sense of confidence in their problem-solving ability and

http://dx.doi.org/10.1037/14936-004
Cognitive Behavioral Therapy Techniques and Strategies, by A. Wenzel, K. S.
Dobson, and P. A. Hays

optimism that they will be able to handle challenges and adversity as they arise.

Cognitive behavioral therapists address problem solving in session from two standpoints. First, they evaluate the degree to which clients possess adequate skills to solve problems. If the therapist detects a skills deficit, then he or she might coach the client in acquiring problem-solving skills. In some instances, clients have adequate problem-solving skills, but they lack skills to implement the desired solution (e.g., an ineffective communication style). In these cases, cognitive behavioral therapists will help the client to acquire the necessary skills to maximize the likelihood that the implemented solution will be successful. Techniques to address skills deficits are discussed in the first section of this chapter.

In other cases, clients have adequate problem-solving skills, but they have unhelpful attitudes or a *negative problem orientation* about problems that interfere with the execution of problem-solving skills. In the second section of this chapter, we describe specific manifestations of a negative problem orientation, how this orientation decreases the likelihood of effective problem solving, and ways to modify a negative problem orientation.

Finally, cognitive behavioral therapists encounter clients who are in difficult situations for which there is no solution (e.g., terminal disease, racism). Problem solving in these instances shifts to a focus on ways in which clients can tolerate these life circumstances in a way that is life enhancing, rather than self-defeating. Cognitive behavioral therapists also work with clients to achieve acceptance of aspects of their life experience that are out of their control. These topics are considered in the third section of this chapter.

Skills Deficits

When a client reports that he or she is overwhelmed or feels "stuck" in life circumstances, cognitive behavioral therapists entertain the possibility that the client is characterized by a problem-solving *skills deficit.* Clients with problem-solving skills deficits do not have the knowledge or ability to effectively solve problems. There are many ways to assess problem-solving skills deficits. Formal assessment can include self-report inventories. One well-established self-report inventory related to problem-solving attitude and ability is the Social Problem Solving Inventory—Revised (SPSI–R; D'Zurilla, Nezu, & Maydeu-Olivares, 2002). The SPSI–R is a 52-item inventory that assesses the degree to which a person possesses tendencies to use the rational problem-solving skills described in this section, as well as the tendency to revert to an impulsive–careless or avoidant problem-solving style and the degree to which the person is characterized by aspects of a positive and negative problem orientation.

Cognitive behavioral therapists also assess for a problem-solving skills deficit in an informal manner, such as by asking the client how he or she would go about solving a current problem or by observing the manner in which he or she attempts to solve problems. It is especially important to gather information about the manner in which the client has approached problems in the past. If clients provide evidence that, historically, they have had difficulty finding or implementing solutions to problems, then the therapist likely would help to develop their problem-solving skills. In contrast, if the client was able to solve problems in the past, it may be that a negative problem orientation interferes with the application of adequate problem-solving skills. In this case, the therapist would use the techniques described in the next section of this chapter. However, it is equally as important to consider alternative hypotheses, such as the effects of recent changes that would preclude the use of previously learned problem-solving skills. In this case, a focus on redeveloping problem-solving skills would be in order.

Two eminent cognitive behavioral therapists, Thomas D'Zurilla and Arthur Nezu, developed an entire cognitive behavioral treatment package that was focused on what they call rational problem solving (see Nezu et al., 2013). Many cognitive behavioral therapists who use problem solving are heavily influenced by this approach and incorporate problem-solving strategies into their treatment plan. In the sections that follow, we describe and illustrate the four steps of problem solving included in D'Zurilla and Nezu's approach.

PROBLEM DEFINITION

The first step in problem solving is to identify, define, and understand the problem(s) at hand. When clients report that they are overwhelmed and stuck, they often know they have problems and can feel their effects, but they have not truly sorted them out. These clients benefit greatly from coaching in problem definition and identification of the key components of their problems. Key tasks in problem definition are (a) seeking available facts about the problem, (b) describing the facts in clear language, (c) separating facts about the problem from assumptions, (d) setting realistic goals, and (e) identifying obstacles to overcome in reaching these goals (Nezu et al., 2013).

It is easy for clients and therapists alike to skip this step because they often perceive their problems to be self-evident. We highly recommend against this practice; a vague or abstract conceptualization of a problem makes it difficult to effectively apply the remaining steps of problem solving. Moreover, conditions such as anxiety and depression are associated with an overgeneral memory style (Williams et al., 2007), which can lead to difficulty retrieving specific memories, which in turn impedes problem solving (Pollock & Williams, 2001) because people with this cognitive style have difficulty recalling the ways in which they solved problems in the past. Our experience is that clients with an overgeneral memory style are also vague when they define their problems, and they need guidance in honing in on specific issues for which a solution can be implemented.

Recall that Shane reported a number of interpersonal difficulties that interfered with his ability to form meaningful connections with potential romantic partners. In the following dialogue, Shane's therapist helps him to move from the general problem of "can't get a girlfriend" to the specific problem of identifying an effective strategy for inviting a particular attractive woman out for a date.

Therapist: [setting the agenda] Shane, what did you hope to accomplish out of today's session?

Shane: I'm just really sick of getting rejected, you know? It's like the whole world is against me. I'm not ugly. I'm not a bad person. Why am I the only person who can't get a girlfriend? It's like rejection is my middle name.

Therapist: You've mentioned a couple of pieces here—that sense of rejection and what it does to your self-esteem and your strong desire to develop a romantic relationship. Which piece would be best to focus on?

Shane: The girlfriend thing. I just really need to figure out what I'm doing wrong and a way to make it work.

[Therapist proceeds to identify other items for the agenda, finalizes the agenda, and moves onto the first agenda item that Shane prioritized—successfully cultivating a romantic relationship.]

Therapist: So if were to describe the problem succinctly, what words would you use?

Shane: [looks dejected] I don't have a girlfriend. I want one. It never works out. Period.

Therapist: Fair enough. It strikes me that this is a big problem with many components. Is it OK if we break it down into smaller pieces?

Shane: Yeah, I think that would be wise. The whole issue just overwhelms me at this point.

Therapist: Which pieces do you think are the most important in this problem?

Shane: [thinking] Well, I don't have much luck with getting that much interest when I ask girls if they want to go out on a date, you know, like for coffee or something. But even when a girl does agree to go out with me, I usually do something to screw it up. So she doesn't *stay* interested either.

Therapist: Ah, two important points. How to get a woman interested in the first place and how to maintain her interest once it is there.

Shane: Exactly. I'm just pretty inept all the way around.

Therapist: Which one of these more specific problems should we tackle first?

Shane: I guess how to get someone interested. I have to have interest before I can keep it, right?

Therapist: That's a good point. Yes, let's focus on your troubles with this first step in forming romantic relationships. [pausing] I'm wondering if we can focus our discussion on one particular situation so that we can translate our therapeutic work into action that can be taken in the near future. Is there a specific woman you're interested in right now?

Shane: [looks down sheepishly] Yeah, there is. She . . . she's a barista at the coffee shop that I stop at every morning before I go to work. I've been wanting to ask her out for a long time now.

Therapist: Great. So let's focus, specifically, on how to approach this woman in a way that maximizes the likelihood that she would agree to go on a date with you.

Shane: Alright.

GENERATION OF ALTERNATIVES

Once clients have clearly identified the problem to be solved, they work with their therapist to generate a pool of possible solutions. This process is typically referred to as *brainstorming.* The idea behind brainstorming is that clients are encouraged to identify as many possible solutions as they can without prejudging them. The suspension of judgment is crucial in this process because many clients (particularly those who are depressed) immediately dismiss potential solutions and endorse the many reasons why the solution will not work. Dismissing potential solutions in this manner has the potential to deprive clients of the opportunity to give serious consideration to solutions that may very well be effective. Thus, not only does brainstorming allow clients to compile a vast pool of potential solutions, it is also an important exercise in remaining non-judgmental and keeping an open mind. Brainstorming also serves as an excellent assessment tool for the cognitive behavioral therapist because it allows a glimpse at how the client derives and evaluates potential problem solutions.

A now classic study published more than 60 years ago determined that most humans are able to keep seven bits of information in working memory (plus or minus two; Miller, 1956). Because clients might identify more than five to seven potential solutions to their problem, it is impor-tant to write down potential solutions so that they do not get lost in the brainstorming process. Ideally, clients will record potential solutions to facilitate their ownership over the exercise, but therapists can also record potential solutions if this is the client's preference.

Shane had some difficulty with brainstorming potential solutions without judgment, as well as identifying a large pool of solutions from which to choose. In the following dialogue, notice the manner in which his therapist dealt with his tendency to dismiss potential solutions, as well the way in which she helped him to identify resources that would supplement his brainstorming of solutions to future problems.

Therapist:	Should we work toward identifying some possible ways to approach this woman?
Shane:	Yeah, that would be very helpful. I'm at a loss.
Therapist:	What ideas come to mind?
Shane:	Ideas? I have no ideas! That's what I'm coming to you for! All I've done so far is wait for her to ask me to go out, and that hasn't worked.
Therapist:	[remaining calm and encouraging in the face of Shane's defensiveness] Believe it or not, you actu-ally identified one possible solution. Waiting for her to ask you out.
Shane:	But I just *told* you, it's not working.
Therapist:	But it's still a potential solution. One thing I've found in my experience, as I work with my clients to solve their problems, is that it's important to consider *all* possible solutions even if they seem outlandish or like they won't work.
Shane:	Why? That makes no sense.
Therapist:	I agree that, on the surface, it might seem counter-intuitive. But I've found that when clients truly

keep an open mind and explore many possibilities, they stumble upon viable solutions that they might not have considered, had they dismissed them outright. For example, some clients take aspects of two or more potential solutions and combine them into something greater than its parts.

Shane: I don't know about that. It seems like a waste of time.

Therapist: How about this—would you be willing to try it out, just this once? And if it ends up being a waste of time, we can certainly do something differently as we work toward solving other problems in your life. Rest assured, you will get an opportunity to evaluate the viability of these solutions after we finish brainstorming. [pause] Are you game?

Shane: OK. I guess so.

[The therapist asks Shane to write down "Wait for barista to ask me out on a date." He identifies another potential solution—asking her out to dinner the next time he frequents the coffee shop. However, he was unable to identify any other potential solutions.]

Shane: I'm at a loss. I really don't know what else to do other than ask her out for dinner the next time I am there ordering coffee.

Therapist: Understood. Let me share something I'm wondering about. Do you have any male friends who are single and looking to get in a relationship?

Shane: Um, sure. My friend Kevin. He got dumped by his girlfriend a few months ago and is looking to get back into the scene.

Therapist: How might Kevin handle this situation?

Shane: [chuckles] He'd be way more smooth about it. He'd probably time it so that he ordered coffee when she was about to take a break. And then he'd ask if he could sit with her, and he'd get to know her more. And from there, he could ask her out. It would flow better than just asking her when ordering coffee.

Therapist: Hmmm, I wonder if that's another potential solution? To see if you can talk with her during her break, and then ask her out in a more natural way?

Shane: [shakes head] I'm not sure if I can pull that off, though.

Therapist: Remember, we're not judging here. We're simply laying out possible solutions.

Shane: OK, I'll write it down.

Therapist: It occurs to me that thinking of ways one friend, Kevin, would approach this gave us another real possibility. How might some of your other friends handle this dilemma?

Shane: [thinking] Probably in a lot of different ways. My friend Doug, he's a real creep—he'd probably hang around until the shop was closing almost like he was stalking her. But my friend Jim . . . yeah, now that I think about it, he may be onto something with his approach. He made a lot of small talk with the person who is now his girlfriend, you know, finding out what she was interested in and then chatting her up about those interests each time he saw her. When he was finally ready to ask her out, they had already been laughing and flirting, so it was pretty obvious that they were going to end up together.

Therapist: Great thinking, Shane! So how many potential solutions do you have here?

Shane: Let's see—waiting for her to ask me out, asking her out to dinner when I get to the front of the line to order coffee, wait until she takes a break and ask if I can sit with her, [laughing] stalking her at the end of her shift, and finding about her interests and talking about them before asking her out. So five different options.

Therapist: You've done some terrific work here, Shane. What I find interesting is that, at first, you had trouble identifying options other than asking her out in line when you were ordering coffee, but then we've ended up with a number of other options. How did that happen?

Shane: Asking me what my friends would do was helpful. They've done some good things. Well, some of them, like Doug, they've done some bad things too. But it helps to get out of my head by thinking of ways my friends would deal with this.

In this dialogue, Shane's therapist relied heavily on solutions that his friends might identify. In reality, there are many ways that cognitive behavioral therapists help to loosen clients' thinking during brainstorming and encourage them to see alternative perspectives. For example, clients can consider how any person might approach a potential problem, whether that person is a friend, classmate, acquaintance, a public figure, or even a fictional character. Therapists might ask what the client would *not* do to solve the problem in the interest of facilitating consideration of opposite approaches. In instances in which clients continue to have difficulty brainstorming potential solutions to problems, cognitive behavioral therapists can ask permission to make some suggestions. However, they typically follow with a question like, "How do you think I knew to make that suggestion?" Such a question can lead to discussion of other resources that can help clients generate alternative solutions to problems.

DECISION MAKING

Decision making occurs when clients arrive at a specific solution or combination of solutions to their problem. Cognitive behavioral therapists encourage their clients to make systematic and thoughtful reflections as they engage in the decision-making process. In many instances, this systematic and thoughtful reflection takes the form of an analysis of the advantages and disadvantages of various options. One common way to conduct this analysis is to have clients draw a grid with three columns—a column for each potential solution, the advantages associated with each solution, and the disadvantages associated with each solution.

Table 3.1 shows Shane's advantages–disadvantages analysis. He was able to identify advantages and disadvantages associated with each of the five potential solutions. At times, he recognized that some of the advantages and disadvantages carried particular weight; in these instances, he designated them as IMPORTANT. He also identified one disadvantage that he considered to be relative minor, so he designated that with MINOR IMPORTANCE. Many clients find that various advantages and disadvantages carry different weights, so it is important to identify a system to capture their relative importance. Using this analysis, clients begin to estimate, realistically, the likelihood of various solutions achieving their desired outcomes.

On the basis of his advantages–disadvantages analysis, Shane recognized that he would feel most comfortable asking the barista out on a date if it flowed naturally from conversation, rather than out of the blue when he was paying for his coffee. He decided that he would begin to make small talk with her when he was paying for his coffee, discussing current events and making comments about any of her interests or opinions that were readily apparent. Because he also recognized that having

TABLE 3.1

Sample Advantages–Disadvantages Analysis

PROBLEM: Don't know how to get a date with barista

Potential solution	Advantages	Disadvantages
Wait for barista to ask me out.	There is no risk of rejection. It would be clear that she is interested in me.	I'd probably be waiting indefinitely. (IMPORTANT)
Ask her out when I order coffee.	I can ask anytime because I order from her almost every day. I'd overcome my fear of rejection.	It might put her on the spot or embarrass her in front of the other customers. I'd feel awkward in front of other customers, so I probably would not come across well. (IMPORTANT)
Ask to sit with her during her break, get to know her, and ask her out on a date.	It would be a nice way to get to know her better. I'd have more privacy when I actually ask her out. (IMPORTANT)	She could think it is strange that I am asking to sit with her during her break.
Hang around until the shop closes and ask her out before she leaves.	I'd have more privacy when I actually ask her out. (IMPORTANT)	She could think I am creepy if I hang around until the shop closes. I would not feel right about doing this. (IMPORTANT)
Make small talk with her when I order, get to know her interests, and ask her out at a time when it flows.	It would be a nice way to get to know her better. It would not seem awkward if I asked her out during small talk about common interests. (IMPORTANT)	It might take a long time for me to establish this kind of relationship with her. (MINOR IMPORTANCE)

some privacy when asking her out was important to him, he decided that after he was more comfortable with her as a result of interacting through small talk, he would then ask to join her during her break and, at that time, ask her out on a date. Thus, Shane arrived at a problem solution that combined elements of two of the potential solutions, even though one might have been dismissed by his quick judgment about his ability to "pull it off."

In other instances, cognitive behavioral therapists recognize the importance of having a Plan A as well as a backup plan, or a Plan B. The presence of a backup plan helps clients to avoid becoming discouraged if their desired solution does not ultimately solve the problem. Moreover, it reinforces the message that there is often no one "right" way to solve a problem, promoting cognitive flexibility about problem solving.

SOLUTION IMPLEMENTATION AND VERIFICATION

A logical homework exercise for clients who are acquiring problem-solving skills is to implement the solution in between sessions. If this type of homework makes sense for a given client, cognitive behavioral therapists encourage their clients to identify the specific time when they will implement the solution and then mentally rehearse the steps they will take to implement the solution (i.e., *imaginal rehearsal*). They also work with their clients to identify any obstacles that could interfere with solution implementation and ways to overcome those obstacles.

Sometimes it becomes apparent that a client lacks the skills to successfully implement the solution. For example, a client might prepare to solve a social or interpersonal problem but lack effective communication skills. In these instances, cognitive behavioral therapists work with their clients to acquire and practice these skills in session as a means of preparation to implement the solution in between sessions for homework. Shane, for example, was concerned that he would embarrass himself while making small talk with the barista when he ordered coffee, decreasing the likelihood that she would be interested in going on a date with him.

Shane: I mean, I feel good that I have a plan now. But I don't totally trust myself to execute it the right way. My friends, like Kevin and Jim, they are much savvier than I am. They're witty. They can think on their feet. Sometimes when I talk to women, I get this sense of panic, and I don't know what to say. I look like an idiot.

Therapist: Would it be worth it to practice making small talk?

Shane: Yeah, I guess so. But I'm not sure it will help. Conversation is spontaneous. We can't script it out.

Therapist: You're right, conversation *is* indeed spontaneous, and scripting it out has the potential to make it a bit awkward or rigid. From my experience, though, if we practice these kinds of interactions here in session, then you will gain some confidence and can build on those success experiences. It doesn't have to be scripted on paper. You can practice right here, in an experiential manner.

Shane: Yeah, OK, I get it. But how do I start? What do I even talk about?

Therapist: What is your sense of what many people talk about at this time of year?

Shane: I guess the weather. Everyone at the coffee shop was talking about the snowstorm last week. . . .

But I don't want to be one of those guys who talks about the weather. How loser-y!

Therapist: But you just hit on an important point—you heard what others were talking about at the coffee shop. And if they are all talking about the weather, why would it be so "loser-y" for you?

[Shane shrugs. Therapist chooses not to pursue restructuring of this unhelpful cognition in the interest of seeing through the problem-solving intervention in its entirety. She makes a mental note to revisit this issue in the future.]

Therapist: Fair enough for now. So let's think. What were are some other topics of conversation that people discuss this time of year.

Shane: [pausing to think for a moment] There's a TV hanging in the corner, so sometimes people talk about what is showing at that moment. Maybe something about a guest on a talk show. Of if the news is on, like a plane crash or something, than people are talking about that. Oh, wait. I know something I can talk about. The basketball tournament is on. And I'm pretty sure that she likes basketball—I think she might have gone to one of the schools that is in the tournament.

Therapist: Those are all terrific ideas, Shane. Especially the basketball idea because basketball is something that you are passionate about as well.

Shane: [looking more optimistic than he has since he started treatment] You know what, this could actually work. I have a few ideas in my back pocket. I usually just go in cold, and I can't think of anything to say when I am put on the spot.

Therapist: Would it be worth it for us to do some practice?

Shane: OK.

Shane and his therapist proceeded to use role-play as a vehicle for him to acquire some conversational skills. First, his therapist obtained a sampling of his skill level, such that he played himself, and she played the role of the barista. Then she asked Shane to evaluate the strengths and weaknesses of his communication approach. Shane recognized that the topics of conversation were appropriate but that he tended to abruptly shift to a new topic of conversation if he did not know what to say next, making the conversation a bit awkward. His therapist suggested that they reverse the role-play, such that she played the role of Shane, and that he played the role of the barista, so that she could model for him appropriate skills for maintaining small talk and transitioning from one topic to another. She gave Shane the opportunity to clearly articulate the skills that he was acquiring to consolidate learning, and they then assumed their original roles in a subsequent role-play that allowed Shane to continue to practice honing his skills. Thus, the acquisition of skills is much more than a therapist telling a client what to do; instead, it is a cycle of practice, reflection, feedback, and honing (Wenzel, 2013).

Despite quality coaching in the acquisition of various problem-solving skills, outside factors may affect the degree to which this implemented solution is successful. For example, neither the therapist nor the client can control whether a potential romantic partner is interested, and it is possible that the client can approach a problem with great skill but yet still get rejected or experience "failure" in terms of the desired outcome. Thus, cognitive behavioral therapists help clients prepare for these outcomes so that they do not become overly discouraged or hopeless about their ability to solve problems. Therapists can approach solution implementation as a "win–win" situation. On the one hand, if the solution achieves its desired effects, then the client has successfully learned and implemented problem-solving skills. On the other hand, if the solution does not achieve its desired effects, then the client can still take credit for the effort, even while he or she learns to tolerate disappointment and adversity. Or sometimes the client might learn about additional skills to be honed in treatment. In other words, the client can view an instance in which he or she failed to solve a problem as an important learning opportunity.

Of course, after the client has attempted to implement the solution for homework in between sessions, it is important for the cognitive behavioral therapist to turn attention toward *solution verification*, or a consideration of the degree to which the solution was successful. It is logical to put review of homework on the agenda of the next session. In addition to allowing clients to discuss the manner in which they implemented the solution, they can consolidate what they learned from the experience and what they will use in the future to solve additional problems that they may face. Consider the following dialogue with Shane, which took place in the session after he had attempted to make small talk with the barista.

> *Therapist:* I've been looking forward to our session to hear how things went when you initiated small talk with the barista. Can you fill me in?
>
> *Shane:* [more animated than he has been in the past] Well, yeah, it went alright. A basketball game was playing on the TV in the corner. It wasn't a game with

her old school, but it was basketball. So I asked her if she was rooting for anyone in the tournament. She was very nice about it and talked about how much she looks forward to this time of year.

Therapist: That's terrific, Shane.

Shane: Yeah, but here's the thing. During our conversation, she mentioned that her fiancé played on the basketball team in college. Can you believe it? She's *engaged*! I never noticed the ring on her finger!

Therapist: Oh! I'm sorry to hear that she is engaged, but you still took a big step forward with your interpersonal problems by initiating this conversation.

Shane: [grinning] But that's not all. The woman behind me heard us talking, and she jumped into the conversation. It turns out that she is a huge basketball fan, too. And we both like the same team. We had so much fun talking that we decided to sit down together and continue chatting. I even got her phone number!

Therapist: [smiling as well] Oh goodness, this was certainly a lively trip to the coffee shop. What did you learn from all of this?

Shane: If I start with topics I am comfortable with, then it's more likely to go well. And, I didn't have to really think of what to say with the woman behind me. It just happened spontaneously. So, I think I need to work on just being my authentic self and not trying to go out of my way to impress women.

Therapist: That sounds like a philosophy everyone can live by.

Negative Problem Orientation

A *problem orientation* is a set of interrelated beliefs that a person has about problems that are encountered in life and one's ability to cope with those problems. People who have a *negative problem orientation* are characterized by the following tendencies (Nezu et al., 2013):

- They view problems are threats, rather than challenges or opportunities for growth.

▪ They view problems are insolvable, rather than solvable.

▪ They doubt their ability to solve or cope successfully with their problems, rather than having a sense of self-efficacy regarding their ability to solve or cope with problems.

▪ They become emotionally distressed when facing their problems, rather than understanding that negative emotional reactions are part and parcel of the problem-solving process.

A negative problem orientation can interfere with problem solving in a number of ways. It is easy to imagine that most people would procrastinate addressing a problem if they view the problem as a threat, believe that there is no solution, doubt their ability to cope with it, and expect uncomfortable emotional distress if they face it. A negative problem-solving orientation can also interfere with the application of the problem-solving skills described earlier in the chapter because a pessimistic outlook can exacerbate depression and anxiety, which in turn can increase concentration problems and fatigue and decrease motivation. In short, when a person has a negative problem orientation, he or she experiences problem solving as akin to "pulling teeth."

The cognitive restructuring skills described in Chapter 4 of this volume can be used to identify and modify a negative problem orientation. For this specific purpose, cognitive behavioral therapists can use the following steps. First, they educate their clients about a negative problem-solving orientation and its effects on problem solving, and they ask whether anything in the discussion "rings true." Next, they work with their clients to identify specific unhelpful beliefs about problems (e.g., "I'm the only one who has problems" or "I'm weak because I have so many problems"). After one or more specific unhelpful beliefs about problems have been identified, cognitive behavioral therapists use guided questioning to help their clients evaluate the accuracy and utility of their beliefs. Exhibit 3.1 lists some common questions that cognitive behavioral therapists can ask to stimulate critical evaluation of these beliefs. After considering their responses to the guided questions, if clients agree that their belief is inaccurate or unhelpful, they then develop a modified belief that is more balanced and factual. Clients can write down this balanced belief and read it when they attempt to solve problems in their lives to bring a balanced problem orientation to their attempt at problem solving.

Ajit, introduced in Chapter 1, had a unique manifestation of a negative problem orientation. Although he firmly believed that he was an effective problem solver, he became agitated in instances in which he believed that he should not have to deal with a problem because of the mistakes or lack of follow-through of others. When this aspect of his problem orientation was activated, he engaged in self-defeating

EXHIBIT 3.1

Guided Questions to Facilitate Modification of a Negative Problem Orientation

- What evidence supports that belief? Is that evidence factual? Is there any evidence that is inconsistent with that belief?
- What is the effect of viewing problems so negatively? What would be the effect of bringing a more balanced orientation to your problems?
- Have you ever encountered a problem in your life that, when solved, brought many positives to your life? [if yes] What does that tell you about problems?
- Have you ever experienced unexpected benefits from having a problem? [if yes] What does that tell you about problems?
- Who else do you know who has problems? Do you judge them in a negative light because they have problems? [if no] What makes you hold yourself to a different standard?
- What advice would you give to a friend who had a similar view of problems?

behavior, such as lashing out at the employees of his company and drinking heavily, which ultimately had an adverse impact on the efficiency with which his company was able to address the problem at hand. Consider this dialogue, in which Ajit and his therapist addressed this aspect of his problem orientation.

> *Ajit:* [becoming agitated] It's just ridiculous! When I tell team members to do something, they need to listen to me and do it. Not tomorrow. Not next week. *Now!* I have enough problems on my plate with having to drum up new business and maintain relationships with my clients. I can't afford to deal with stupid problems that result from others' incompetence.

> *Therapist:* [with empathy] Yes, it sounds like you have some extra work that you didn't expect to have on your plate. Can we pinpoint what button, exactly, that this situation triggered in you?

> *Ajit:* The utter incompetence of my employee. That I now have to clean up the mess that he created. [shaking his head] I can't take it.

> *Therapist:* Tell me if you think this is accurate. It sounds to me that you have the belief that there should not be problems caused by the mistakes or lack of follow-through of others. What do you think?

> *Ajit:* [pausing] Well, yeah! If everyone did their job as I told them to do it, I wouldn't be in this situation in the first place.

Therapist:	When something happens that violates that belief, like the incident yesterday, what is your emotional reaction, and how intense is it?
Ajit:	My emotions go through the roof. Anger, frustration, anxiety, disgust—all of it.
Therapist:	I wonder if, together, we can take a look at this belief and see if there is a way to soften it up.
Ajit:	[exasperated] You mean I have to just accept that my employees are going to drop the ball? That everything will always fall into my lap?
Therapist:	No, not at all. However, my theory is that when this standard you have is violated, you have a very intense emotional reaction that ends up being self-defeating. For example, yesterday, how did you respond when you learned of the problem?
Ajit:	[puts head in hands] Not good. Not good at all. I screamed at the guy who dropped the ball, calling him incompetent. Then I stormed out of the office and had five glasses of scotch. And I missed my first two conference calls of the morning. [pausing] Yes, I know. I know that it ends up being self-defeating.
Therapist:	How realistic is it to never have problems due to another person's mistakes or lack of follow-through?
Ajit:	It's unavoidable. I know that I can't expect others to do things exactly like I do. That's why I'm the CEO, and they're working for me. Not the other way around.
Therapist:	And the effect of holding onto this belief that you shouldn't have to deal with problems due to others' mistakes or lack of follow-through?
Ajit:	The effect is substantial. If I'm honest with myself, I know I've lost people because of the way I've treated them when they screw up. And that really makes me feel bad, in hindsight. I pride myself on developing young talent, so I don't want them to leave with negative feelings about their experience in my company.
Therapist:	I wonder if we could adjust this belief so that it's a bit softer and more balanced?
Ajit:	[thinking] I think I have to realize that, in the majority of instances, my team is really great. But

mistakes are inevitable. I guess that's part of the territory of being CEO—handling mistakes smoothly and gracefully.

Therapist: That sounds quite balanced to me. The old way of thinking is that problems should not occur ever. The new way of thinking is that your team actually performs well most of the time, that occasional mistakes are inevitable, and that you're equipped to handle them as the CEO, even if they are frustrating.

Ajit: Yes, exactly.

Therapist: How much do you believe the new way of thinking?

Ajit: I believe it 100%.

Therapist: Let's apply it to yesterday's incident. When you view the incident with the new lens, what is the intensity of your anger, anxiety, and disgust?

Ajit: It has decreased a lot. Actually, it's making me think that I should go to the office after the appointment and apologize to the guy I yelled at to make things right.

Therapist: You've done great work here, Ajit. Should we turn our attention to figuring out how you will remember this the next time you are faced with a mistake that causes you extra work?

Acceptance

There are many instances in which clients skillfully apply problem-solving skills and adopt a positive, proactive attitude toward their problems, yet continue to be unable to solve their problem. Cognitive behavioral therapists encourage clients to accept circumstances that they cannot change or are beyond their control. In this instance, the problem at hand shifts to ways that clients can tolerate, accept, and grow from circumstances that are less than ideal.

Some clients dislike the idea of acceptance, equating it with resignation. In contrast, cognitive behavioral therapists encourage clients to let go of a desire to force change on something that cannot be changed, identify ways to achieve personal growth, and live a quality life despite the existence of the problem. For example, a client with terminal cancer might not be able to change the fact that he will likely die within the next several years. However, he can focus on gratitude for the experiences he has had in his life and attempt to live his last years in a meaningful way that is consistent with his values. The renowned psychologist Marsha Linehan regarded *radical acceptance* as complete acceptance of a problem or undesirable life circumstances, letting go of fighting against circumstances that cannot be changed (e.g., Linehan, 2015). She distinguished between *willfulness*, a cognitive orientation characterized by denying that a problem exists, refusing to accept that it cannot be changed, and doing everything in one's power to control it, and *willingness*, a cognitive orientation characterized by allowing one's circumstances to be what they are and engaging with those circumstances, rather than retreating or fighting against them. In other words, acceptance is a stance that clients can take proactively in a way that conveys strength and wisdom.

Acceptance plays a role in problem solving for the two cases discussed in this chapter. Shane, for example, had to accept that the barista is engaged to be married. Had he not had the fortunate experience of meeting another desirable woman, his therapist would have worked with him to accept this fact, tolerate his disappointment, and acknowledge the growth that he achieved by learning problem solving and communication skills and taking a risk. Ajit had to accept that his team members will not always perform as he would. This acceptance was reflected in the more balanced belief about problems that he constructed, such that he acknowledged that problems are a part of most companies and that part of his role is to solve them.

Conclusion

"Real-life" problems are a common focus of treatment in CBT, as many clients believe that problems cause or exacerbate their emotional distress. Cognitive behavioral therapists assist with problem solving in three ways: (a) acquiring and practicing problem-solving skills, as well as skills to implement the solutions arrived at during problem solving; (b) identifying and modifying a problem orientation that interferes with the ability to execute effective problem solving; and (c) achieving acceptance and tolerance of problems that are outside of their control.

Cognitive behavioral therapists who help their clients to acquire problem-solving skills are often influenced by the pioneering work of D'Zurilla and Nezu (Nezu et al., 2013). In this approach to problem solving, clients are taught problem definition, generation of alternatives, decision making, and solution implementation and verification. In many instances, it becomes apparent that clients lack the skills to implement solutions effectively, so cognitive behavioral therapists also work with them to acquire skills such as assertiveness or interpersonal effectiveness. When a negative problem orientation affects clients' ability to become motivated to solve problems or focus on the problem-solving process, cognitive behavioral therapists help these clients identify unhelpful beliefs about problems and craft a new belief that is more balanced, accurate, and helpful.

Cognitive behavioral therapists take a broad view in their definition of problems. A problem could be something straightforward, such as bills that are due when a client does not have enough money to pay them. However, a problem could also be clinical issues themselves, such as recurrent panic attacks or lack of acceptance of an estranged relationship with another person. From this perspective, all of the cognitive behavioral strategies described in this volume can be used in the service of addressing the problems associated with clients' emotional distress.

Cognitive Restructuring of Automatic Thoughts

4

ognition lies at the heart of the cognitive behavioral model. According to this model, the way in which we think about, interpret, or judge our life circumstances plays a large role in how we feel about those circumstances. When people engage in negative thinking about their lives, it is logical that they experience aversive emotional reactions, such as depression, anxiety, guilt, or anger. People who seek out psychotherapy often experience challenging problems in their lives, and their aversive emotional reactions are understandable. However, it is just as often the case that these people limit their focus on the negative aspects of their problems or exaggerate the importance of those negative aspects, which in turn exacerbates their emotional distress and can interfere with problem solving.

The next two chapters describe *cognitive restructuring*, or the process by which cognitive behavioral therapists help clients to *identify* aspects of their thinking that have the potential to be overly negative or limited in scope, systematically

http://dx.doi.org/10.1037/14936-005
Cognitive Behavioral Therapy Techniques and Strategies, by A. Wenzel, K. S. Dobson, and P. A. Hays

evaluate the accuracy and helpfulness of that thinking, and *modify* that thinking into a more balanced appraisal of their problems. In this chapter, we focus on cognitive restructuring of *automatic thoughts*, or thoughts that are experienced when a person is faced with a particular situation or set of circumstances. As clients gain skill in noticing and modifying these situation-specific automatic thoughts, they begin to notice patterns or themes that point to an underlying belief that they hold about themselves, others, or the way the world works. Cognitive restructuring of these underlying beliefs is discussed in the next chapter.

Introducing Cognitive Restructuring

As with any cognitive behavioral strategy, it is important for the therapist to establish a sound rationale for the intervention so that clients can see the powerful role that their cognition plays in their emotional distress, as well as the powerful role that the modification of cognition can play in recovery from emotional distress. The take-home message for clients is that although they may face challenging situations in their lives, it is the way that they perceive and the meanings that they attach to these situations that are especially important to address in therapy. Cognitive restructuring can help clients to derive accurate, helpful, and balanced situational interpretations and meanings. Many cognitive behavioral therapists find it useful to illustrate these principles with examples from clients' lives and have some pre-prepared examples that illustrate the role that cognition plays in emotional reactivity. Consider this dialogue, in which Beth's therapist educated her about the association between cognition and emotion and provided a glimpse about the potential value of cognitive restructuring.

> *Therapist:* I've noticed throughout our work together that when you face a stressful situation in the classroom, your mind automatic goes to thoughts like, "I'm a horrible teacher." Is that a fair observation?
>
> *Beth:* Yes, definitely. I think those things all the time.
>
> *Therapist:* What is the effect of thinking in that way?
>
> *Beth:* Well, it just makes me feel horribly about myself, of course. And I'm paralyzed. Just so paralyzed in the very situations where I need to step up and take control.

Therapist: I have an idea that might help. What would you think of a strategy that can help you catch yourself when you start to go down that road of negative thinking and use some tools to ensure that you're thinking in the most balanced way possible?

Beth: I think I could benefit from that, yes. But how do I do that?

Therapist: The idea is to remember the meaning that we make out of situations that we face in our lives, rather than the situations themselves, are associated with the emotional reactions that we experience. In your case, when you are faced with a crisis in the classroom, your mind goes to, "I'm a horrible teacher." And then you feel depressed and anxious, and your ability to problem solve in that moment decreases. But what if your mind went to a more balanced place? Something like, "I've handled situations like this before, and they've generally gotten resolved." What emotional reaction would you associate with that sort of statement?

Beth: But that isn't true. I don't handle crises well. I really *am* a horrible teacher.

Therapist: [choosing not to question directly the notion that Beth is a horrible teacher at this point in the session] Let's take a hypothetical situation and see how we can apply it to the problems you face. Are you OK with that?

Beth: Sure.

Therapist: Consider Scenario A. A person is at the mall and sees a neighbor walking in the opposite direction. She attempts to make eye contact with the neighbor, and the neighbor turns away. The first thought that jumps into her mind is, "My neighbor is trying to avoid me." If that was her first reaction, what emotional reaction might she have?

Beth: Um, if she's anything like me, she'd be mortified. She'd be really down on herself.

Therapist: And if she's mortified and down on herself, how might she act toward the neighbor the next time she sees her?

Beth: She'd probably avoid the neighbor. You know, like not go outside when everyone in the neighborhood is socializing. That sort of thing.

Therapist: And would be the effect of doing that avoidance?

Beth: [pauses] It would probably make her life more difficult. She'd be so self-conscious she wouldn't want to go outside.

Therapist: Yes, that's right. But now let's consider Scenario B. A person is at the mall and sees a neighbor walking in the opposite direction. She attempts to make eye contact with the neighbor, and the neighbor turns away. The first thought that jumps into her mind is, "Oh, she must not have seen me. I know she has a lot on her mind." If *that* was her first reaction, what emotional reaction might she have?

Beth: She wouldn't be as depressed or mortified. She probably wouldn't feel anything. She'd just let it go.

Therapist: And if she took that stance, how much she act toward her neighbor the next time she sees her?

Beth: Like nothing ever happened. Maybe she wouldn't even remember it.

Therapist: What would be the effect of that type of thinking?

Beth: She certainly wouldn't imprison herself in the house like the other person.

Therapist: Exactly. What are you concluding from this example, Beth?

Beth: I get it. I really do. That our thinking can get us into a lot of trouble. But, my situation seems more real. There *have* been plenty of times that I haven't handled a crisis well. I *did* get a negative performance review by the principal.

Therapist: I understand. We certainly don't want to sugar coat problems that have their basis in facts. At the same time, I can't help but wonder if, at times, the things that you say to yourself in these situations are not terribly helpful, and they contribute to the vicious cycle of stress and inaction in which you find yourself.

Beth: Yes, I think you're right. I always go to the extreme, and my anxiety goes from 0 to 10 in a manner of seconds. That's not good for anybody.

Therapist: Would you like some help in dealing with these thoughts?

Beth: Very much so.

In this example, Beth's therapist first attempted to illustrate the way in which cognitive restructuring works with an example from her own life. However, Beth was unable to loosen her thinking about her perceived incompetence, so her therapist instead turned to a hypothetical example to illustrate the associations among thinking, emotion, and behavior, as well as the way in which changing one's thinking affects the other areas. In many instances, clients can grasp more fully the tenets of the model when they are distanced from their own life circumstances. Over time, clients begin to accept the model, and to view their own automatic thoughts in a more nuanced manner.

Beth's therapist carefully emphasized the association between negative thinking and self-defeating behavior (i.e., ignoring the neighbor in the future) and balanced thinking and adaptive behavior (i.e., continuing to behave normally around the neighbor). When clients realize that cognitive restructuring can help them to make sound decisions that will ultimately be in their best interest, they usually invest themselves in the model and increase their commitment to practice. In addition, notice that Beth's therapist assured her that he was not giving her the message that she should "sugar coat" problems that have their basis in facts. Clients can be assured that cognitive restructuring is not the same thing as positive thinking because positive thinking has the potential to be just as inaccurate as negative thinking. Instead, clients are told that cognitive restructuring helps them to acknowledge all of the information that affects their life problems and to recognize that some of those pieces might not be as negative as they are concluding. In other words, cognitive restructuring encourages *balanced* thinking.

Identifying Automatic Thoughts

The first step in cognitive restructuring is to help clients to recognize and put words to their automatic thoughts. Although it is easy to view this step as self-evident, more often than not, clients need to develop skill to identify the most relevant automatic thoughts that account for most of their emotional distress. Some useful questions that help to identify automatic thoughts include the following (cf. J. S. Beck, 2011):

▪ What was running through your mind in that situation?
▪ What would you guess had been running through your mind in that situation?
▪ If [a family member or friend] were in that situation, what might run through his or her mind?

■ Did you experience a mental image of a future catastrophe? Or a bad memory from the past?
■ Might you have been thinking _____ [supply a thought that seems appropriate for the situation and the client's emotional distress] or _____ [supply a thought that seems to be the opposite of that which would be expected for the situation and the client's emotional distress]?
■ What did that situation mean to you? Or mean about you?

Notice the mental imagery question. Some clients experience automatic thoughts as images, rather than as words that run through their minds. Cognitive behavioral therapists must be mindful that automatic thoughts might not be experienced as statements that clients explicitly say to themselves. Other clients who have difficulty identifying their thoughts can be asked about the meaning that the situation holds for them or about them. Such clients might recognize that they are viewing the situation through a negative "filter" that might not be stated overtly in their minds but that nevertheless colors the manner in which they are interpreting the situation. That filter then serves as the automatic thought to be subjected to cognitive restructuring.

Beth was easily able to identify the most central automatic thoughts associated with her emotional distress when she began to practice cognitive restructuring. In contrast, Ajit had more difficulty. The following dialogue illustrates some of the common problems that cognitive behavioral therapists encounter when they are helping clients to identify automatic thoughts.

Ajit:	I tried to apologize to the guy, and he gave me attitude. I blew up at him all over again.
Therapist:	Tell me, when your employee responded to you in that way, what ran through your mind?
Ajit:	[annoyed] My mind? I don't know. Nothing. I didn't have time to think. I just blew my top.
Therapist:	In my experience, when we have an abrupt emotional reaction to something, there is usually some meaning that we are making out of that situation, even if we're not entirely aware of it.
Ajit:	OK. I guess I was like "Really? How dare he? *I'm* the CEO. I *gave* him this opportunity to be in the company."
Therapist:	That's true. You are the CEO. You did recruit and hire him fresh out of his master's program with little work experience. So what does all of this mean?

> *Ajit:* [thinking] He's disrespecting me. He's ungrateful. If others see that he can treat me that way and get away with it, then I've lost control of the whole company.
>
> *Therapist:* These are very powerful thoughts indeed. He's disrespecting you. He's ungrateful. And his behavior could lead to you losing the whole company. Would it be OK with you if we took a closer look at these thoughts?
>
> *Ajit:* OK.

Several points about this dialogue deserve note. First, it is common for clients to indicate that they do not know what was running through their mind or to view their emotional distress as immediate and not associated with any thoughts or images. Although this indeed occurs on some occasions, clients more often simply need practice to slow down and recognize the presence of these thoughts and images. Cognitive behavioral therapists tell clients that automatic thoughts are so named exactly because they often come about so quickly that people do not always know that they are present and exerting effects on mood and behavior. Clients who do not know what is running through their mind typically need to practice this step of cognitive restructuring.

Ajit also demonstrated another common occurrence when clients first learn to identify automatic thoughts, as he provided a surface-type "gut" reaction (i.e., "Really? How dare he?"), rather than the true meaning of the situation. Although reactions like this may well constitute the first reactions that occur to clients, it is difficult to identify a more balanced response to such reactions. In Ajit's case, he proceeded to provide more details about the situation (i.e., that he is the CEO of the company, that he gave the employee the opportunity to work there) that were factual in nature. In both of these instances, cognitive behavioral therapists inquire about the meaning underlying the "gut" reaction or the additional description to identify the significance of the situation to the client. It is that significance that can then be subjected to cognitive restructuring.

When cognitive behavioral therapists use time in the therapy session to teach clients to identify automatic thoughts, it is often logical to continue to track automatic thoughts between sessions as homework. Although, in principle, this exercise can be completed by clients in their head, by paying attention to their thoughts, we strongly encourage some type of record of the clients' automatic thoughts. When clients first learn cognitive restructuring and try to identify automatic thoughts without writing them down, they characteristically have difficulty recalling the essence of their cognitive, emotional, and behavioral reactions when they return to session several days later. As with any other new skill, it is usually prudent to approach the capture of automatic thoughts in a slower, more progressive and detailed manner at the beginning, and then move toward more efficiency once the basic skill has been acquired.

A standard tool that clients can use to record automatic thoughts is a *thought record*, historically known as the Dysfunctional Thought Record. The thought record is a structured template in which clients record their automatic thoughts when they notice an increase in emotional distress. The thought record in Figure 4.1 includes four columns so that clients can write down problematic situations, automatic thoughts, emotional responses and their intensity, and behavioral responses. This format allows clients to see the relations among their automatic thoughts, emotions, and behavior. However, many clients find that it is cumbersome to record these data on a thought record and prefer methods that they view as more convenient, such as using a Microsoft Excel spreadsheet, the notes function in their smartphones, or the voice recording function on their smartphones. Some smartphone apps have been developed to record key elements contained in thought records. Clients are more likely to complete the thought record and bring more fulsome information into therapy when they are able to use their preferred method for homework, so some discussion of this issue with the client is likely valuable.

FIGURE 4.1

Situation	Automatic Thought	Emotional Response	Behavioral Response
Briefly state the facts describing what happened.	What thought ran through your mind? What did it mean to you?	What feeling did you experience, and how intense was it? 0 = *not intense* 10 = *the most intense I can imagine*	What did you do in response to the automatic thought?

Basic thought record.

Evaluating Automatic Thoughts

Once clients can identify automatic thoughts associated with their emotional distress, they can begin to evaluate the accuracy and usefulness of those thoughts. Here, the cognitive behavioral therapist uses *Socratic questioning*, which is a guided and systematic questioning to stimulate critical thinking about the automatic thought and to allow clients to draw their own conclusions about the accuracy and usefulness of the thoughts. Initially, the therapist will pose Socratic questions to clients so that they learn to answer these questions and draw different conclusions about their life circumstances. Eventually, cognitive behavioral therapists expect that clients will learn to apply these questions on their own without the help of a therapist. This process of asking and answering Socratic questions is called *guided discovery*. Research shows that for every standard deviation increase in the use of Socratic questioning with any one depressed patient, there is a corresponding decrease of approximately 1.5 points on the Beck Depression Inventory—II report at the time of the subsequent session (Braun, Strunk, Sasso, & Cooper, 2015).

Evidence questions are those that are posed to help clients thoroughly evaluate the accuracy of their thinking (J. S. Beck, 2011) by weighing the evidence that supports their automatic thought and the evidence that is inconsistent with their automatic thought. Consider this dialogue between Beth and her therapist in which they evaluated the automatic thought, "I don't have what it takes to be a special education teacher."

Therapist: Give me some specific examples to support the idea that you don't have what it takes to be a special education teacher.

Beth: I can never handle a crisis, that's for sure.

Therapist: Let's take a closer look at that statement. When you say you can "never handle a crisis," that suggests to me that every single time something happens that is out of the ordinary, you have been unable to handle it. Is that true?

Beth: Well, no, I guess not every time. But *most* of the time.

Therapist: Is it OK if we look at this as factually as possible?

Beth: OK.

Therapist: Today is Monday, so you've had one full day in the classroom this week, yes? [Beth nods.] Can you walk me through the events of the day and identify each instance in which something unexpected happened that you needed to handle?

Beth: Oh gosh, that's a lot, it seems like there are always unexpected things happening. But I guess this morning was pretty quiet, relatively speaking. The only thing out of the ordinary was that one of the students had a bathroom accident, and we had to change his clothes. [Therapist writes down "bathroom accident."] But this afternoon got crazy. Two of the kids lost it, and we had to restrain them. One of them got cut during the incident and started bleeding, so I had to write up an injury report. My assistant teacher had a family emergency that she needed to attend to, so I was left in the classroom all by myself for the last hour of the day. And a parent of one of the quieter children called to complain that her son was being bullied by another student, so I had to deal with her right after school. It almost made me late to this appointment.

Therapist: [looking down at the list he compiled] So it seemed that there were six unexpected incidents that you had to handle today—the bathroom accident, two children needing to be restrained, the injury report, being in the classroom on your own for the last hour of the day, and the phone call to the upset parent.

Beth: Yes, that's right.

Therapist: How did you handle these incidents?

Beth: The bathroom accident was no big deal. I just cleaned it up and changed his clothes. With the children who needed to be restrained, one was mine, and one was the assistant teacher's.

Therapist: It must be difficult to manage instances when children become violent. How did this one go?

Beth: Not great, but I managed to quiet him down. It was the other child who was more out of control and got cut.

Therapist: Were you the one who completed the injury report?

Beth: I have to because I'm the main teacher.

Therapist: And how about the last two incidents, when you had the classroom on your own and when you returned the phone call of the upset parent?

Beth: I was pretty worried about what would happen if something went horribly wrong when I was on my own. Luckily, I had the materials for a very easy arts and crafts project that is a favorite. It kept them busy and out of trouble. And the phone call . . . the mother was angry, understandably, but she seemed satisfied that I would be on the lookout for bullying in the future.

Therapist: Hmm. So you had six unexpected incidents happen to you today, five of which required that you take the lead in handling it. And it seems to me that you did handle each one of those, am I right?

Beth: [looks shocked] I never thought to look individually at each incident. I just focus on the big ones, where I drop the ball.

The turning point in Beth's cognitive restructuring work occurred when her therapist asked her to focus on specific evidence. To that point, she had concluded that she could "never" handle a crisis. Thus, a key task in therapy is to shift from sweeping generalizations to specific instances, which allows clients to accumulate a rich data set as the basis for conclusions about the accuracy of their thinking. Cognitive behavioral therapists are alert for "evidence" that is not truly factual. For example, Beth identified "never handling a crisis" as a piece of evidence to support the notion that she did not have what it takes to be a special education teacher. It was only after guided questioning that she realized that this piece of evidence was overstated. Another common pitfall that cognitive behavioral therapists often encounter is clients' dismissal or the discounting of evidence that is inconsistent with a negative automatic thought.

An *attribution* is an explanation that a person makes for situations or problems. For example, if a person fails an exam, he might attribute it to being stupid (i.e., a maladaptive attribution about himself), or if a person interviews for a job but does not get it, she might attribute it to her job references, who perhaps said negative things about her (i.e., a maladaptive attribution about others). *Alternative explanation questions* can help clients see that, in most cases, many factors come together to explain why a situation occurred, and that only a small piece of the equation is something being bad about them or other people. These questions help clients to soften self-blame and self-deprecation, as well as to curb anger toward other people or circumstances. Ajit's therapist used alternative explanations to address his anger toward his employee, who he viewed as disrespecting him.

Therapist: Ajit, you're attributing the attitude that your employee demonstrated this morning to being disrespectful and ungrateful. But I'm wondering if there might be other explanations for his behavior.

Ajit: Other explanations? Like what, he wasn't feeling well or something? I don't buy that for a minute.

Therapist: Fair enough, if he didn't seem ill or off to you, then that's probably not a valid explanation. But here's something I'm wondering. You said he's young, right?

Ajit: Yeah. He's 24, fresh out of a master's program.

Therapist: And you said he's also very ambitious, correct?

Ajit: Yeah. [smiles] He actually reminds me of myself when I was that age.

Therapist: Ah, well, consider this. Let's say you were in this situation when you were a young, ambitious 24-year-old. How would you react if your boss came at you in a way that seemed a bit over the top?

Ajit: I . . . probably . . . wouldn't have liked it very much.

Therapist: Would you have handled it gracefully, or maybe not so much?

Ajit: I get your point. I probably wouldn't have handled it very well. I was so cocky that I probably would have taken it ever further. Like walked out, never to return.

Therapist: What does this tell you?

Ajit: [sighs] I get it. That he responded to me out of immaturity, not necessarily out of overt disrespect.

Therapist: Since you're putting your 24-year-old self in his shoes, can you think of yet another reason for why he might have acted as he did, aside from being disrespectful of you or simply being immature?

Ajit: Well . . . I remember when I was in college and doing a summer internship. The boss was a real jerk, and it seemed that he targeted me specifically. Sometimes I had to dish it right back to him because I felt like I had to protect myself.

> *Therapist:* That sounds like a tough situation. How does that translate to you and your employee?
>
> *Ajit:* I never thought of it that way. He probably feels threatened when I get on him for making a mistake. So then he needs to save face and try to stand up to me.

Cognitive behavioral therapists frequently come across clients who engage in what is called *catastrophizing*. When a person catastrophizes, he or she estimates an unrealistically high likelihood of the occurrence of a worst-case scenario and assigns an overly high cost to that scenario. The person then takes as fact that this worst-case scenario will indeed occur, that it will be devastating, and that he or she will not be able to cope with or recover from it. Evidence questions can help these clients put their concerns into perspectives. However, another approach is to use *decatastrophizing questions*, in which therapists ask clients to estimate the realistic likelihood that a worst-case scenario will occur; consider how bad, realistically, it would be if a worst-case scenario were to occur; and how they would cope if a worst-case scenario were to occur. Consider this dialogue with Shane, who struggled with the automatic thought that he would be rejected if he were to pursue the woman with whom he connected at the coffee shop.

> *Shane:* I was about to call her, and I just couldn't bring myself to do it. I just can't take the rejection.
>
> *Therapist:* OK, so here's that same idea at work again—that you'll be rejected. Is it safe to say that's the worst-case scenario?
>
> *Shane:* Yeah, there's nothing worse than that.
>
> *Therapist:* But what's the best-case scenario?
>
> *Shane:* That's easy. That I call her, ask her out, she says yes, and we really hit it off.
>
> *Therapist:* And what about the most realistic scenario?
>
> *Shane:* Realistically? Man, I don't know. I guess that she'd probably go out with me? Because she was the one who initiated the conversation? And then sat down with me for over a half an hour to talk about basketball?
>
> *Therapist:* Ah, interesting. What do you notice about how the most realistic outcome lines up with the best- and worst-case scenarios?
>
> *Shane:* The most realistic is pretty much the same as the best. [pauses] But what if she says no? I don't think I can take that.

Therapist: I think it's worth considering the worst-case scenario a bit more. Imagine that she does decide that she's not interested in seeing you again. How would you cope?

Shane: [shakes his head] Yeah, that's the thing. I'm feeling fragile right now. I feel like if someone rejects me *again*, after all of these rejections, that it would push me over the edge.

Therapist: What does going "over the edge" mean?

Shane: That I would lose hope. Who knows what would happen then?

Therapist: So, for you, rejection might not relate to just this one relationship, but to a loss of hope. No wonder this situation is so scary for you. Do you think it would be worth it for us to put together a coping plan that can help you get through the disappointment if she says she does not want to go out to dinner with you?

Shane: I think that would be a good idea.

Although decatastrophizing questions can help clients realize that the probability of a worst-case scenario is typically low, it is important for clients to accept that safety, acceptance, and desirable outcomes cannot be guaranteed. Thus, it is also important to help them to see that they have the coping resources to deal with adversity or disappointment, to diffuse the magnitude of meaning that these worst-case scenarios carry.

As stated previously, clients sometimes find it difficult to apply systematic reasoning skills because they are entrenched in the throes of emotional distress. *Distancing questions* help clients to apply Socratic questions to situations outside of their own, which presumably are associated with less personal meaning than their own situations. In most cases, clients see that they would be much kinder to others than they would to themselves, as they would judge others less harshly than they would judge themselves. When this cognitive pattern is identified, cognitive behavioral therapists ask clients to explain the discrepancy between the standards they hold for themselves and the standards they hold for others. In addition, cognitive behavioral therapists often pair distancing questions with *impact questions*, such that they encourage their clients to consider the consequences of holding unrealistic standards for themselves, or more generally, the consequences of a pessimistic or apprehensive thinking style. Many clients begin to see that there is great cost to thinking in such an unhelpful way and that it interferes with the goals they hope to achieve.

Cognitive behavioral therapists undoubtedly encounter circumstances in which clients are facing a problem that most people would find difficult and aversive and that their thinking about the problem is accurate and as balanced as it can be, given the undesirable circumstances. In these cases, there is no need to encourage clients to change their thinking. Instead, cognitive behavioral therapists ask *problem-solving questions* to help these clients consider ways to cope with or solve the problem at hand. Consider this dialogue with Ajit, who continued to sense tension with his employee even after apologizing for yelling at him.

Therapist: How did it go when you apologized to your employee?

Ajit: [shaking his head] Not good, I think. I think he's still really upset. I'm not sure the apology made any difference.

Therapist: How do you know that?

Ajit: He was looking down, not making eye contact. Giving me a lot of one-word answers. The past few days, it's seemed like he's watching the clock for five o'clock to arrive, and he hightails it out of there without saying goodbye to anyone.

Therapist: And you're concluding that he's still upset.

Ajit: Yeah. And that I've done some damage. The thing is, he plays a key role in the company right now, so it's important that he's comfortable with the company and that he'll stick around for a while. I know he's not going to be perfect; I accept that. But we all have to be on the same page so that we can work as a team.

Therapist: So you've accepted that he's not perfect, and you're also concerned about how he's functioning with the team in light of the tension.

Ajit: [sinks back in chair] Yeah, exactly.

Therapist: Well, it seems like you have a good handle on the situation. What can you do about it?

Ajit: I think I should do something to show him how valued he is. I try to have development meetings with each of my employees every few weeks. He and I haven't met for a while. I could take him somewhere nice for lunch and give him the opportunity to openly express any remaining concerns he might have.

Therapist: Sounds like you have a good approach. I wonder if you and I should also plan for ways for you to handle any negative feedback that you might receive from him.

Modifying Automatic Thoughts

If the results of the evaluation suggest that a client's thinking is inaccurate, exaggerated, or otherwise unhelpful, then the cognitive behavioral therapist helps the client modify the automatic thought into a *balanced thought*. A balanced thought incorporates all of the conclusions that were drawn from the evaluation questions into a coherent response to the automatic thought. Automatic thoughts tend to be short, pointed, and overgeneralized, whereas balanced thoughts are lengthier and nuanced to take into account the complexities with which most life circumstances present.

Balanced thoughts need to be compelling to be effective in times of emotional distress. Most clients find that balanced thoughts that simply dismiss the original automatic thought (e.g., "Just get over it" or "Everything will be OK") are not believable in the moment when they are overwhelmed by the automatic thought. Thus, balanced thoughts are typically at least a few sentences long and acknowledge the factual basis of the original thought, but they incorporate the evidence that is inconsistent with the automatic thought, other explanations for the circumstances that the client is facing, or steps the client is going to take to solve the problem. Table 4.1 lists some automatic thoughts and their corresponding balanced thoughts.

After clients have crafted their balanced thought, cognitive behavioral therapists ask them to rerate the intensity of their emotional distress using the same scale as they rated the intensity of their emotional distress associated with their original automatic thought. This step is essential in that it provides objective evidence that the cognitive restructuring process has been successful in reducing the intensity of clients' emotional distress. A rule of thumb is to ensure that the balanced thought is associated with no more than a mild level of emotional distress (e.g., a 3 on a 0-to-10 scale, with 0 being the absence of emotional distress, and 10 being the greatest amount of emotional distress that the client can imagine). When clients construct balanced thoughts but then assign a level of emotional distress that is greater than a 3, cognitive behavioral therapists help them identify associated automatic thoughts to which the information included in the balanced thought might now apply. In the following dialogue, consider the way in which Shane's therapist handles this type of situation.

> *Therapist:* Your original automatic thought was "I'll be rejected," and you rated your anxiety as being a *10* out of 10 on our 0-to-10 scale. Now that we've worked on this a bit, what's a more balanced way of viewing this situation?

TABLE 4.1

Sample Balanced Thoughts

Client	Automatic thought	Balanced thought
Beth	I can never handle a crisis.	There have been some times when I froze in the face of a crisis in the classroom. But today, six things happened that were unexpected, and I handled every one of them, including an instance in which a child became violent. I do deal OK with the majority of crises in my classroom. I can seek guidance from more experienced teachers on ways to handle the truly scary crises.
Ajit	My employee is disrespectful and ungrateful.	My employee is only 24 years old and probably responded like he did more out of immaturity than disrespect. When I lost it on him, he probably felt threatened, so he needs to give me attitude to save face. The best thing to do is accept that he is not perfect and apologize, given the important role he plays in the company.
Shane	I will be rejected.	I do think I have a good shot with this woman. After all, she was the one who started a conversation with me. And we got along real well when we were having coffee. Yes, the pain of rejection will sting in the short term. But I have a plan to get through that. The pain of not trying is worse in the long term.

Shane: I do think I have a good shot with this woman. After all, she was the one who started a conversation with me. And we got along real well when we were having coffee. [voice trails off]

Therapist: I'm sensing a "but" there. Am I correct?

Shane: Yeah, you got me. I know we just developed this coping plan in case she doesn't want to go out with me. I don't know, though, I still feel like it will be devastating if it doesn't work out.

Therapist: So when you say to yourself, "I have a good shot with this woman. After all, she was the one who started a conversation with me. And we got along real well when we have having coffee," on our 10-point scale, how anxious are you?

Shane: Still like a 6. Because the rejection could still happen.

Therapist: Fair enough. I think we need to add a piece to the balanced thought that directly addresses the pain associated with rejection. [pauses] Let me ask you this: which pain is worse? The pain of being without a romantic partner and really wanting one, or the pain of being rejected when you are taking steps to reach your goal?

Shane: Hmm, that's tough. I would say the short-term pain of being rejected is worse. But . . . I guess the pain of being lonely and not having a girlfriend is way worse in the long run.

Therapist: Let's add that to the balanced thought. [Shane writes.] Can you read back what you've written? The whole thing?

Shane: OK. I do think I have a good shot with this woman. After all, she was the one who started a conversation with me. And we got along real well when we were having coffee. Yes, the pain of rejection will sting in the short term. But I have a plan to get through that. The pain of not trying is worse in the long term.

Therapist: Now what rating would you give to the anxiety associated with that set of statements?

Shane: Umm, a *3*, I think. I don't ever think I'll get down to a *0*.

Therapist: That's OK. The uncertainty associated with asking someone out on a date would be at least a little anxiety provoking for almost anyone.

Shane: But, I don't know, I guess this makes me feel more optimistic.

Therapist: That's terrific. Do you think it would be helpful to read this balanced thought before calling her to ask her out?

Shane: Definitely.

The thought record in Figure 4.1 can be easily expanded to include space for clients to record balanced thoughts, the associated level of emotional distress, and new behavioral responses. Figure 4.2 is an example of an expanded thought record. After practicing the evaluation and modification of automatic thoughts in session, clients can use the expanded thought record in between sessions to practice generating balanced thoughts in times of emotional distress. They are encouraged to complete the thought record as closely as possible to the time in which they noticed emotional distress so that they can gain practice applying their cognitive restructuring tools in real time, before an overreaction gets the best of them.

FIGURE 4.2

Situation Briefly state the facts describing what happened.	Automatic Thought What thought ran through your mind? What did it mean to you?	Emotional Response What feeling did you experience, and how intense was it? 0 = *not intense*; 10 = *the most intense I can imagine*	Behavioral Response What did you do in response to the automatic thought?	Balanced Thought Evaluate the accuracy and usefulness of the automatic thought and incorporate that information into a more balanced way of viewing the situation.	New Emotional Response Rerate the intensity of the emotion associated with the original automatic thought. List any new feelings that you are experiencing.	New Behavioral Response What did you do differently as a result of the balanced thought?

Expanded thought record.

Clients can practice and reap the benefits of cognitive restructuring using techniques other than thought records. For example, a coping card is a small index card or piece of paper on which clients can record the fruits of their cognitive restructuring work. They can write the automatic thought at the top of the card and their balanced thought underneath it, or they can write the automatic thought on one side of the card and the balanced thought on the other side. When they notice the activation of that automatic thought, they can quickly pull out their card and remind themselves of the balanced way of viewing their situation. This technique works particularly well for clients who (a) experience the same automatic thought repeatedly, (b) need balance and centeredness before doing something scary or aversive, and (c) find the thought record too cumbersome to complete. For example, because Beth frequently experienced the automatic thought "I'm a horrible teacher," she wrote out a coping card with a balanced thought, and she took it out of her purse and read it every time she felt insecure in the classroom. Shane, on the other hand, completed a coping card in response to the automatic thought "I'll be rejected, and I won't be able to take it." He read his coping card immediately before dialing the phone number of the woman he wanted to ask out on a date. At the time of the subsequent session, he told his therapist that doing this indeed helped him to remain calm during the conversation, and he was happy to report that the woman agreed to go out to dinner with him.

Some clients need more specific direction to evaluate their automatic thoughts than they get from a typical thought record. Cognitive behavioral therapists can work collaboratively with such clients to develop a worksheet in which key evaluation questions are posed, and the client is given space to respond to those questions. Figure 4.3 provides an example of such an evaluation worksheet. Although we have chosen some of the most versatile evaluation questions that we use in our own clinical practices, it is important to recognize that any questions can be included in an evaluation worksheet that would be helpful for a particular client to gain distance from and perspective on situations that are associated with emotional distress.

FIGURE 4.3

Situation: _____

_____

Automatic Thought: _____

Emotion: _____ Intensity (circle): 0 1 2 3 4 5 6 7 8 9 10

Behavioral Response: _____

Evidence that supports the automatic thought: _____

_____

Evidence that does not support the automatic thought: _____

_____

What is the best that could happen in this situation? _____

What is the worst that could happen in this situation? _____

If the worst happens, how will I cope? _____

What is most realistic that will happen in this situation? _____

What is the impact of thinking in this way? _____

What is the benefit of changing my thinking? _____

BALANCED THOUGHT: _____

_____

_____

Emotion: _____ Intensity (circle): 0 1 2 3 4 5 6 7 8 9 10

Behavioral Response: _____

Sample evaluation worksheet.

Finally, as stated earlier in this chapter, new mobile phone apps are continuously being developed to facilitate the implementation of many cognitive behavioral strategies, including cognitive restructuring. Clients can locate these apps by typing *CBT* or *cognitive behavioral therapy* in the "search" function at app stores.

Conclusion

Cognitive restructuring is a powerful tool that can help clients to identify, evaluate the accuracy and usefulness of, and modify problematic thinking that exacerbates emotional distress. Clients typically begin to examine automatic thoughts in session with their therapist, and they work with their therapist to devise homework that will allow them to practice the application of skills in their own lives for homework. With practice, clients acquire the ability to modify unhelpful thinking as it occurs, before they experience a substantial increase in negative affect.

The examples provided in this chapter focused on automatic thoughts associated with depression, anxiety, and anger. Although cognitive behavioral therapists commonly work with thoughts associated with these emotional experiences, cognitive restructuring need not be limited to these domains. For example, during a manic phase, clients with bipolar disorder may experience expansive or grandiose thoughts that are associated with elevated positive affect and risky behavior, such as spending a large sum of money or taking on a project that is too large to complete. They can use cognitive restructuring tools to evaluate the accuracy and usefulness of those ideas, perhaps developing a coping card that they can read in the moment when they are at risk of acting on dangerous thoughts. Clients with substance use disorders often report "permission-giving" thoughts (e.g., "It's OK to have a drink because it is a special occasion"), and the application of cognitive restructuring can help them to consider the consequences of engaging in substance use and the reasons for staying sober. Clients with eating disorders often report inaccurate ideas about societal standards of beauty (e.g., "Men only like women who are super skinny"), and the application of cognitive restructuring can help them to realize that such a statement is a sweeping generalization that is not supported by data and to achieve acceptance of their bodies. Thus, according to the cognitive behavioral model, distortions in thinking are a prominent feature of most, if not all, mental health disorders, and cognitive restructuring can be adapted to address whatever manifestation of unhelpful thinking a client reports.

Cognitive Restructuring of Underlying Beliefs 5

According to the cognitive behavioral model described in Chapter 1 of this volume, all people possess underlying beliefs that are formed on the basis of many historical factors, including biological, psychological, cultural, and environmental influences. Many of the environmental influences take the form of formative life experiences. Those key life experiences can be single events, such as a trauma, or ongoing circumstances that reinforce messages about the self, relationships, or about the general operation of the world. Beliefs that are formed on the basis of these messages serve as filters through which people make meaning of their life experiences. Once established, they tend to skew our memories for past events, so that they are consistent with our beliefs, and they also influence the way that we perceive ongoing events, as illustrated in Chapter 4. It is important to acknowledge that beliefs can be healthy, adaptive, and flexibly used. However, cognitive behavioral therapists who see clients with depression, anxiety, and other mental health problems usually focus on negative, unhelpful, and rigidly applied beliefs.

http://dx.doi.org/10.1037/14936-006
Cognitive Behavioral Therapy Techniques and Strategies, by A. Wenzel, K. S. Dobson, and P. A. Hays

Underlying beliefs take two forms. *Core beliefs* are fundamental beliefs about the self, others, or world. Examples of unhelpful core beliefs are "I'm a failure" and "Others are untrustworthy." *Intermediate beliefs* are rules and assumptions about the way life operates. These beliefs stem from core beliefs and are usually rigid and inflexible, which may predispose someone for disappointment when life does not work as expected or when he or she does not live up to the belief. Examples of unhelpful intermediate beliefs are "If I don't get into medical school, then I'm a failure" or "People judge you by how much money you make."

Many clients report significant benefits from the strategies discussed in this volume, such as behavioral activation, problem solving, and cognitive restructuring of automatic thoughts. However, when a person is characterized by one or more pronounced beliefs that continue to be problematic, many cognitive behavioral therapists emphasize belief assessment and modification (e.g., Wenzel, 2012). This chapter describes ways to identify unhelpful underlying beliefs, identify components of the beliefs that are problematic, and modify these unhelpful beliefs into new beliefs that are balanced, compelling, and adaptive.

Identifying Underlying Beliefs

The first step in working with underlying beliefs is to recognize when they are activated and operative. Underlying beliefs are often more difficult for clients to recognize than situational automatic thoughts because many clients experience them as such a central part of themselves that their accuracy is not questioned. Moreover, they are often painful to acknowledge, so there is benefit to not examining or trying to change them.

There are many ways that cognitive behavioral therapists recognize when clients are describing or have stumbled on underlying beliefs. As stated in Chapter 1, J. S. Beck (2011) identified three broad categories of core beliefs: those in the *unlovable* domain (e.g., "I'm undesirable," "I will always be rejected"), those in the *helpless* domain (e.g., "I'm ineffective," "I'm a failure"), and those in the *worthless* domain (e.g., "I am worthless," "I am a waste"). When a client expresses one of these statements, cognitive behavioral therapists who are familiar with these domains will recognize that he or she is likely hitting on a powerful underlying belief.

In addition to fairly simple models such as that proposed by J. S. Beck to identify beliefs, other more elaborate models exist. For example, Young, Klosko, and Weishaar (2003) developed an elaborate models of beliefs (often called *schemas*), which they broke down into five domains and 16 specific schemas (see http://www.schematherapy.com). However, cognitive behavioral therapists in training need not be concerned that they must memorize a list of beliefs and catch them as they become evident in session because there are many other ways to identify underlying beliefs. For example, therapists can help their clients notice the themes associated with their own automatic thoughts, as they occur across the course of several sessions. This deductive strategy was used by Beth's therapist, who reasoned that automatic thoughts such as "I'm a horrible teacher," "I don't have what it takes to be a teacher," and "I'm going to be fired because of my performance" all pointed to an underlying belief centered on the theme of personal incompetence.

To help clients put their own words onto underlying beliefs, therapists ask their clients what conclusions they drawn from the themes that emerge during the cognitive restructuring of automatic thoughts. A commonly used technique to identify core beliefs is the *downward arrow technique*, first mentioned by A. T. Beck, Rush, Shaw, and Emery (1979) and subsequently elaborated on by Burns (1980). Therapists who use this technique ask about the meaning associated with automatic thoughts to the point that the client and therapist eventually get to an idea that is so fundamental that there is no further underlying meaning associated with it. The following vignette depicts the manner in which Shane's therapist used the downward arrow technique to make explicit the core belief associated with the automatic thought that he would be rejected by the woman with whom he was now in the early stages of dating.

Therapist: Shane, I'm so pleased to hear that things are going well for you in this new relationship.

Shane: Yeah, thanks, but I don't know . . . [trails off]

Therapist: Tell me more.

Shane: Well, it's good and all, *for now.* But history tells me that I'm going to screw it up. Eventually, I'll do something to turn her off, and she'll end it.

Therapist: So that idea that you'll be rejected is still floating around in your mind.

Shane: Yeah. There are just too many past experiences where that has happened.

Therapist: It's clear that these experiences carry great meaning for you. [Shane nods his head.] What do they mean about you?

Shane: Mean? They mean I can't keep a girlfriend for very long.

Therapist: Let me play devil's advocate for a moment. Let's assume that this is true—that you're incapable of maintaining a partner relationship—what does *that* mean to you? Or about you?

Shane: [shaking] Well, it means I'm going to be alone my whole life.

Therapist: [gently] And what does that mean about you, if you end up without a romantic partner for your life?

Shane: [visibly distraught] It means no one will ever love me. I'm completely unlovable. What's worse than that?

Therapist: I wonder if we've hit upon a fundamental belief that you have about yourself—that you're unlovable. Do you think this belief colors the way you view relationships in your life?

Shane: Definitely, no question. My parents *have* to love me because I'm their kid. But I know they're disappointed in me. I have some friends, but it's not like they really love me. Especially now that they're all starting their own families. I'm not the person who they would look out for like family. [pausing, looking down, then speaking quietly] I really just want a family of my own, you know? People who will love me unconditionally, who will think I'm great even with warts and all.

Notice the nonverbal indicators of Shane's affect when he was discussing his core belief. He began to shake and look visibly distraught. He paused and averted eye contact. When he did speak, he used a soft tone. In many instances, when clients have arrived at a painful core belief, it is evident by their display of affect. When a client becomes tearful, agitated, or otherwise distressed during cognitive restructuring, this work is often close to a key belief.

Intermediate beliefs are often identified by "if–then" statements. For example, Ajit held the belief that if an employee did not readily agree with him, then the employee was being disrespectful and ungrateful. Beth held the belief that if she could not handle every crisis that crossed her path, then she was an incompetent teacher. Consider the following dialogue, in which Shane's therapist helped him to identify an important intermediate belief about relationships when he had his first disagreement with his girlfriend approximately three months into their new relationship.

Shane: [agitated] See, I told you, I always screw it up.

Therapist: [using a calm, even voice] Let's slow down for a minute. Tell me what happened.

Shane: We couldn't decide what movie we wanted to see. I wanted to see an action film, and she wanted to see a romantic comedy. I don't know why I pushed it; I should have just gone with what she wanted to see. But I really wasn't in the mood. So I pressed the issue, and it started an argument. I ended up just taking her home.

Therapist: OK, so you had your first disagreement.

Shane: But don't you understand? It's over.

Therapist: It's over? How long ago did this happen?

Shane: Last night.

Therapist: And have you spoken since then?

Shane: No, not spoken. I guess we texted a little, but that's it. We usually talk on the phone before bed every night.

Therapist: Let me check something out with you. Could you finish this sentence for me? [Shane nods his head.] Having a disagreement with my girlfriend means . . .

Shane: That it's done! That I did it again!

Therapist: Do you believe that there should be no disagreements in relationships?

Shane: Well, I don't know if I would go that far. Every couple fights once in a while. But, for me, a fight this early in the relationship means that it's over.

Through this discussion, Shane's therapist recognized that he operated according to the intermediate belief, "If we have a fight early in a relationship, it means the relationship is over." Had Shane continued to invest in this belief, he likely would have behaved in a manner that increased the likelihood that this notion would be realized (i.e., a self-fulfilling prophesy). For example, he might have refrained from contacting his new girlfriend or ignored her attempts to contact him, or he might have behaved in a way that put her off the next time they spoke. However, Shane's therapist used cognitive restructuring to help him to see that many outcomes could follow a first fight in a relationship. Once he adopted that more flexible viewpoint, he was able to take action that was effective in repairing and continuing to build the relationship.

Defining Old and New Beliefs

Cognitive behavioral therapists who work with clients to shape old, unhelpful beliefs into new, more adaptive beliefs take care to arrive on thorough definitions of these beliefs. Many clients report extreme, "all-or-nothing" beliefs like "I am worthless" or "I am a failure" and focus their attention on aspects of their lives that are consistent with these beliefs, but they fail to acknowledge aspects of their lives that are going well or are at least not problematic. By spending the time defining the specific components of old and new beliefs, clients begin to understand the overgeneralized nature of these beliefs and gain some perspective; therapists can then identify more precise targets for intervention. Consider this dialogue with Beth, who continued to struggle with the belief that she was incompetent.

Beth: I know in our last visit we were able to see all the things that I do at work to make me an OK teacher. But, I don't know, bad things keep happening. I don't think that I can argue them all away.

Therapist: We had identified the theme of being incompetent as ringing true to you, yes? [Beth nods.] Would it be OK if we took a look at all of the pieces that go into being a competent person? [Beth nods again.] OK, so clearly, being competent on the job is one aspect of being competent. Can you think of others?

Beth: [thinking] Hmmm, I don't know. Paying bills maybe? I guess a person would be incompetent if he let all of his bills pile up.

Therapist: That makes sense. So, managing finances is also a part of being competent?

Beth: Yes, I think so.

Therapist: Anything else?

Beth: Those are the two biggies. I can't think of anything else.

Therapist: Well, how about being competent interpersonally, such as with friends or family members?

Beth: I don't think that's competence, really. I think it's the capacity to love and be loved.

Therapist: Let's take an example. Consider a person who lacks social skills and the ability to understand social cues. This person becomes angry very easily when she misperceives others' intentions. As a result, her relationships with others are highly volatile, and she often cuts people out of her life, or else is held at arm's length by others. How would you assess her social competence?

Beth: Oh, when I look at it like that, I guess social competence *is* pretty important.

Therapist: Ah, so we now have three important areas of competence. Now that we're thinking more broadly about what it means to be competent, can you think of any areas that we have missed?

Beth: How about competence in keeping oneself healthy, both physically and mentally?

Therapist: Yes, most people would agree that those are important areas of competence.

Beth: And I suppose competence can be shown if one has a hobby or interest outside of work, like running or sailing or something.

Therapist: Oh, sort of like your competence in crocheting?

Beth: [looks taken aback] *My* competence? All I do is crochet when I am stressed out and need to focus on something other than my job.

Therapist: And what's the feedback that you get on the pieces that you create?

Beth: [looks sheepish] People really like them. My sister says she's grateful because she is all thumbs and can't figure out how to crochet to save her life.

Therapist: So, part of being competent is having talent and ability in some sort of recreational pursuit outside of one's career.

Beth: Yes, I guess it does. [pauses] And running a household is also a part of competence. Now I'm thinking of my brother. His apartment is such a pigsty, and he gets cockroaches and mice because he never cleans up. I guess that would make him incompetent in that area. And he's also completely clueless when it comes to helping my parents, who are older and have trouble getting around. Whenever I ask him to make a phone call, to help them out, he ends up creating *more* work for me because he does not know how to negotiate the system.

Therapist: Now you're really identifying lots of areas that make up competence. Can we summarize?

Beth: Sure, OK. There's competence on the job. Financial competence. What did we say with other people? Oh yes, social competence. Competence with physical and mental health. Competence in

> hobbies and interests. Competence with running a household. And competence with helping older parents.

Therapist: That's eight areas of competence if we split physical and mental health into two separate domains.

Beth: I never thought about it like this. I was focused only on competence at work.

Therapist: What does this tell you?

Beth: That, at least in some circumstances, I am competent.

Although this exercise was designed primarily to provide more information relevant to Beth's belief of incompetence (which would be used in future cognitive and behavioral interventions), it also had an immediate therapeutic effect. It helped Beth move from a pronounced, inflexible view of herself as incompetent to a more nuanced view of her competence in a number of domains. Notice that Beth initially dismissed some domains as outside of competence (e.g., social competence). However, her therapist applied the principles of cognitive restructuring to help her broaden her view of competence and, in doing so, helped to stimulate her to identify even more domains associated with competence. Cognitive behavioral therapists who help clients define beliefs in this manner often assemble the fruits of their work into a pie chart, such that the "pie" is divided into the many domains that feed into their belief.

Modifying Underlying Beliefs

All of the techniques used to restructure automatic thoughts can be used to modify underlying beliefs. For example, therapists can encourage clients to (a) examine the evidence that supports and does not support the belief; (b) consider other, more benign explanations for key life events that contributed to the development of the belief; and (c) weigh the advantages and disadvantages of keeping the old, unhelpful belief and adopting a new, more balanced belief. In this section, we describe some additional techniques that shift underlying beliefs.

BEHAVIOR CHANGE

At times, cognitive behavioral therapists encourage clients to "lead with their behavior and allow their mind to follow." In other words, when clients make behavioral changes in their lives that are consistent with new and healthier beliefs, they begin to see that these new beliefs have value and are associated with a better quality of life than the old, unhelpful beliefs.

Cognitive behavioral therapists who use this technique first help clients to define specific behaviors associated with the various components that make up a belief. For example, Beth's therapist worked with her to identify behaviors indicative of competence on the job, such as financial management and social relationships. Figure 5.1 lists the specific behaviors that she identified in session. Next, cognitive behavioral therapists work with clients to acknowledge the areas in which they already engage in desired behaviors and areas in which there was a discrepancy between their current behavior and desired behavior. When she reviewed the list depicted in Figure 5.1, Beth realized that she was already competent in managing her finances, maintaining the household, and caring for her elderly parents. She indicated that her mental health was not where she would like it to be, but she acknowledged that she was complying with all of the behaviors that she believed were necessary to address this area of her life. Although she continued to view her performance on the job as severely deficient, she remarked that she was encouraged to have a specific plan that targeted behaviors to improve competence in this domain. Beth recognized that she tended to isolate herself when she felt some depression and anxiety and that she was prone to letting her social contact with others slip, especially after her divorce; thus, she expressed a commitment to attend to this area of her life. She also identified goals for her physical health and hobbies and interests, which she believed would increase her sense of competence in these areas.

Clients can implement systematic behavioral changes to reinforce new and more balanced beliefs over time. In other words, clients commit to aspects of behavior change in the spirit of achieving a change in beliefs. Over the course of several sessions, Beth implemented one behavior a week that targeted her competence on the job, her social relationships, her physical health, and her hobbies and interests. At the time of each session, she evaluated the degree to which her growing behavioral set was affecting her perception of her competence. As treatment progressed, she judged herself as being more generally competent, even as she stated that she lacked some confidence to deal with unruly children in the classroom (although she did acknowledge significant improvement in this area) and that she was not fully where she wanted to be with her diet and exercise. Nevertheless, this new view of her competence was associated with a significant reduction in depression and anxiety, as well as a decreased frequency with which she experienced self-deprecating automatic thoughts about her abilities.

POSITIVE DATA LOG

Clients who keep *positive data logs* record two types of evidence across the course of several sessions: (a) evidence that supports the old, unhelpful

FIGURE 5.1

COMPETENCE	
Job	Handle unruly children without the need for assistance.
	Finish administrative paperwork on time.
	Make creative lesson plans.
	Keep up on latest research on teaching special needs children.
Finances	Pay all bills on time.
	Save for retirement.
Social relationships	Talk to brother and sister at least once a week.
	Maintain regular contact with three closest friends.
	Accept invitations for social outings when extended.
Physical health	Exercise at least three times a week.
	Eat "clean" at least 80% of the time.
	Maintain normal blood pressure, heart rate, and cholesterol levels.
Mental health	Take psychiatric meds as directed.
	Attend weekly therapy sessions.
	Do CBT homework.
Hobbies and interests	Enter crocheted pieces into local competitions.
	Join a knitting group and develop proficiency.
Household	Clean up kitchen each evening.
	Vacuum and dust on weekends.
	Attend to all maintenance issues when they arise.
Care for older parents	Talk to parents on the phone each day.
	Run errands with parents each weekend.
	Fill parents' pill box for the week.
	Make parents' doctor's appointments as needed.

Sample list of behaviors to target for belief change.

belief; and (b) evidence that supports the new, healthier belief. When they identify evidence that supports the old belief, clients are encouraged to use their cognitive restructuring tools to construct a balanced reframe (cf. J. S. Beck, 2011; D. Dobson & Dobson, 2009; Persons, Davidson, & Tompkins, 2001). Beth used this technique in combination the behavioral changes she made. She quickly began to accumulate evidence that supported the belief that she is competent. When she experienced a setback on the job, she recorded the incident in a column of evidence that supported the old belief of incompetence, but she also wrote statements such as, "But this was a truly difficult situation. Most people would require assistance" or "I need to remember that everyone makes mistakes, and mistakes are not equivalent to incompetence, especially if I learn from them."

COGNITIVE CONTINUUM

The *cognitive continuum* is a technique used to modify many of the overgeneralized, all-or-nothing beliefs that have been considered in the chapter to this point, such as being worthless or a failure (J. S. Beck, 2011; D. Dobson & Dobson, 2009; Persons et al., 2001). Cognitive behavioral therapists who use this technique draw a horizontal line on a piece of paper or a white board and designate each end as an extreme on the continuum. For example, the left end of the continuum might be designated as *0%* and labeled *failure*, and the right end of the continuum might be designated as *100%* and labeled as *successful*. Key points in between are also designated, such as *25%*, *50%*, and *75%*. Next, clients indicate where they fall on the continuum, and the therapist makes a mark on the continuum. Clients who experience acute symptoms of depression or other mental health disorders will often rate themselves very low. Then, the cognitive behavioral therapist asks Socratic questions to prompt clients to make more accurate ratings. When clients respond to each question, they revisit their estimate, and the therapist either erases or crosses out the previous mark and makes a new mark on the continuum. This process continues until both the client and therapist concur that they have arrived at an accurate rating. Consider this process with Shane, who continued to struggle with the belief that he was unlovable. At this point in the dialogue, the therapist explained the rationale for the technique drew the continuum, and indicated Shane's initial rating of being *1%* on the continuum from unlovable to lovable.

> *Therapist:* What is the rationale behind your rating?
>
> *Shane:* Well, my parents say they love me. So that makes me higher than a *0*. But I don't think that counts

that much. Parents are *supposed* to love their children. *Everyone's* parents love them.

Therapist: It is true that many, many parents love their children unconditionally. At the same time, I wonder if you're overgeneralizing a bit here. And also dismissing the importance of love that is very real.

Shane: You mean like acknowledging weird instances, like parents who adopt children from foreign countries but then want to send them back when the kids are too much to handle?

Therapist: That's an interesting example. Can you tell me more about how those children compare with you?

Shane: I bet you're trying to get me to say that there are some people, like kids that get sent back to orphanages, who are more unlovable than I am. [Therapist begins to respond.] But I don't see it that way. I think the parents are the ones who don't deserve love in this case. How could they adopt a helpless child, bring that child to a different country, and then reject him? All kids deserve to be loved.

Therapist: Ah! Say that again.

Shane: All children deserve to be loved?

Therapist: Right. Exactly. Every single one of us was a child. So what does that tell you?

Shane: That maybe there isn't truly anyone who is unlovable?

Therapist: I think you might be onto something. How much do you believe that?

Shane: [pauses] I do. Even murderers on death row have mothers who love them and stand by them, right?

Therapist: So I wonder if there is a chunk of the continuum that is not even relevant, given that all human beings deserve love and are truly lovable to others.

Shane: Yeah, I think you're right. Let's cross out the last 25% of the continuum.

Therapist: [crossing out the last 25% of the continuum] Now we have a range that runs from 25% to 100%. Where would you put yourself on that continuum now?

Shane: Well, I guess if murderers on death row would be at 25%, I'd have to be higher. I haven't done anything that would truly make me repulsive to other people or that have hurt other people. So people *can't* reject me for those reasons. Maybe, I don't know, in between 30% and 35%? Let's go with 33%.

Therapist: When you say to yourself, "I am 33% lovable and 67% unlovable," how do you feel?

Shane: Still not very good. It still seems that almost everyone else is higher.

Therapist: Shall we continue to examine this notion?

Shane: OK.

Therapist: I wonder if it's accurate to say that your parents are the only ones who love you.

Shane: I guess not. My sister does. And her boyfriend, I don't know if he loves me, but he's definitely on my side. I suppose my brother, too, although he's another one who probably loves me because he has to, rather than because he wants to.

Therapist: Well, let's not dismiss your brother just yet. And what about extended family members?

Shane: Well, yeah, there are a bunch of them. I'm real close with my uncle, although I think I burden him with all of my issues. And my grandparents. Three of my four grandparents have passed away, but we had a real nice relationship.

Therapist: What kind of picture are you painting here, Shane?

Shane: OK, OK. So there are lots of family members who love me, or at least have loved me before they died.

Therapist: What rating on our continuum would you assign now?

Shane: I guess maybe 60%. I have more family than most people, if you count extended family. And we're all pretty close. [pauses] But it still seems like there is this part of me that's unlovable. I can't seem to get or keep a girlfriend.

Therapist: What have been your most significant romantic relationships in the past?

Shane: I've had a few girlfriends in the past, but no major relationships. I dated for a few months in the spring of my last year in high school. We went to prom together. But then it was pretty clear that we had to break up because she was going to college across the country, and we would never see each other.

Therapist: Hmm, this is interesting. How long did the relationship last, then?

Shane: For about four months I guess. I think we started dating that March, and we broke up in the summer, around July.

Therapist: And the decision to break up sounds like it was more due to circumstances than it was to something you did, yes?

Shane: [pauses] I guess you're right. I mean, I would have stayed together with her, but she wanted her freedom at college. [pauses again] But, I guess we didn't break up because I messed up. It probably would have happened sooner or later because of the distance.

[Therapist continues to ask questions about the length of Shane's previous relationships and the circumstances under which they ended. Two of his additional four relationship partners genuinely seemed to care about him and other reasons, rather than his undesirability, seemed to account for the greatest proportion of variance in the ending of that relationship.]

Therapist: Now we've considered the family members who love you, as well as some aspects of your most significant romantic relationships. What rating on our continuum would you assign now?

Shane: Now it *has* to be higher than a 60%, right? I'm still not going to give it a 100%, though, because I have so much trouble meeting women these days.

Therapist: Fair enough.

Shane: I guess I'd give it an 80%.

Therapist: What a change that is from 1%. [Shane nods.] When you rate yourself as being 1% lovable, how does that affect your confidence when you're trying to establish a romantic relationship?

Shane: Oh, it's horrible. Like why bother?

Therapist: And how do your confidence and your behavior change when you rate yourself as 80% lovable?

> *Shane:* I'm so much better. I actually have some hope that it will work out. And that would make me relax because I'm not so worried all the time about making a mistake.

HISTORICAL TEST OF CORE BELIEFS

Cognitive behavioral therapists who facilitate the historical testing of underlying beliefs invite clients to examine the validity of their beliefs at various time periods in their client's life, such as during childhood, high school, college, young adulthood, middle adulthood, and so on (cf. J. S. Beck, 2011; Persons et al., 2001). This technique helps clients to see that there is usually a great deal of evidence from previous periods of their lives that are inconsistent with their underlying belief and that they likely ignore or dismiss this evidence. Moreover, it helps clients to see the origin of unhelpful beliefs and put in perspective those key events that contributed to the development of those beliefs. Consider the following dialogue, in which Ajit's therapist used this technique to evaluate the accuracy of the belief that he was a "one-hit wonder" and made a great accomplishment on one occasion that could never be replicated.

> *Therapist:* This idea of being a "one-hit wonder" has come up a great deal in our therapeutic work.
>
> *Ajit:* [puts his head in his hands] I know, I know. I just can't shake it. My father's words are etched in my brain.
>
> *Therapist:* Would it be OK if we took a look at the accuracy of that notion in your life?
>
> *Ajit:* Sure.
>
> *Therapist:* The year you won the prizes in each of the six academic subjects—that was fourth grade, yes?
>
> *Ajit:* That's right.
>
> *Therapist:* What about in the other grades? Did you win no prizes?
>
> *Ajit:* No, I always won prizes. One year I won prizes in two of the six areas; in another year, I won prizes in four of the six areas. But never six out of six again. And that was what disappointed my father.
>
> *Therapist:* [putting aside, at the moment, questioning related to Ajit's perception of his father's disappointment] So is it fair to say that you always won *some* of the prizes in each year of elementary school? [Ajit nods his head.] Tell me how the rest of your schooling

proceeded before you came to the USA for college. Were there other academic contests? Contests of other sorts?

Ajit: Well . . . I ended up graduating first in my class.

Therapist: So you were valedictorian?

Ajit: Yes, in a sense, it doesn't work quite like that in India. But I was the equivalent of the valedictorian.

Therapist: That sounds quite impressive to me. In fact, I wonder if you had two big "hits"—winning all six prizes in fourth grade and graduating at the top of your class in high school?

Ajit: [smiles] I guess you could put it that way.

Therapist: What about in college? Did you stay a "two-hit wonder" then?

Ajit: Probably. I wasn't really into college. I was bored, actually. So I did just enough to get by while I was trying to lay the groundwork to establish my own company.

Therapist: But you went to an Ivy League school, yes?

Ajit: Well, yes.

Therapist: Do you think many people would view being admitted to and graduating from an Ivy League school as two more "hits"?

Ajit: [taken aback] I never thought of it that way. I think it was just assumed in my family that I would go to a top university in the U.S.

Therapist: By my count, we're now up to four big "hits," plus a number of smaller "hits" when you won various prizes in the other grades. Would you agree?

Ajit: [becoming excited] Yes, I would definitely agree. I've spent so long focusing on my next business conquest that I've forgotten about some of these important milestones in my past.

Therapist: Would it be worth it to continue to examine your big and small "hits" during your adult years?

Ajit: Yes, definitely. [Ajit goes on to identify two major accomplishments, as well as many smaller accomplishments, that he had achieved in his career.]

Therapist: What do you conclude from all of this?

Ajit: I guess I can't be a "one-hit wonder." I've had a number of "hits" in my life.

Therapist:	So if the old belief is "I'm a one-hit wonder," the new belief is what?
Ajit:	Um, "I'm very accomplished." Yeah, I guess that's accurate. [pauses] I don't know, though, the future is so uncertain. I'm not sure what's going to happen with this company. What if there's nothing else for me?
Therapist:	Ah, that's a different issue entirely. Perhaps we should focus on two things. One would be developing tools to weather uncertainty. [Ajit nods his head.] And the other would be to, perhaps, diversify your activities a bit so that you are not solely invested in the success of your company. Many of my clients find that when they engage in a range of valued activities, if one area of their life is not going so well, the other areas can carry them through and give them meaning.
Ajit:	Yes, that's exactly what I need to do. I need to have a few "hits" going at the same time.

RESTRUCTURING EARLY MEMORIES

Some clients benefit from experiential exercises, in which they "relive" early events that contributed to the development of unhelpful beliefs and apply their cognitive restructuring tools to gain perspective on these beliefs when associated painful affect is elicited (J. S. Beck, 2011). This experiential technique is particularly useful when clients believe "intellectually" that their unhelpful beliefs are inaccurate but when they continue to tie themselves to these beliefs "emotionally" in the face of a stressor or a disappointment. This technique can be especially useful for clients who appear to intellectually understand the idea of belief change but just do not feel it at a deep or "core" level.

Therapists who use the technique often begin by using vivid imagery to help clients think back to and experience the affect associated with a past experience that reflected the main theme associated with the belief. Clients are instructed to close their eyes (if they are comfortable with doing so) and describe the event that contributed to the development of the belief using the present tense. Consider the manner in which Ajit's therapist conducted this exercise with him when he linked the belief of being a "one-hit wonder" back to his perception of his father's disappointment in him. This dialogue began after his therapist secured his permission to participate in the exercise. Ajit closed his eyes and assumed the role of his fifth-grade self, one full year after he won all six prizes.

Therapist: You won all six prizes last year in fourth grade, and now the awards ceremony for fifth-grade prizes is occurring. Tell me what is running through your fifth-grade mind.

Ajit: I really want to win all six prizes again. Two years in a row! No one has ever done that before.

Therapist: And tell me what happens in the ceremony.

Ajit: I win the first prize for mathematics. But then the science prize comes up. It goes to someone else, someone I really dislike. I realize that I am not going to win all six prizes this year.

Therapist: And how do you feel, emotionally?

Ajit: I am sick to my stomach. I know that my father is going to be disappointed in me.

[Therapist continues to elicit subsequent events, thoughts, and emotions throughout the rest of the ceremony and on Ajit's walk back home.]

Therapist: You walk in the door, and what happens?

Ajit: [talking softly] My father immediately asks me what happened at the awards ceremony and whether I won all six prizes. And I say, "No, Father. This year I won the prize for mathematics and history." [lip trembling] And my father says, "Why not all six prizes this year, boy? You must not be working as hard. Maybe you need a tutor. If this continues, you'll never get into a top university in the US."

Therapist: What's running through your mind right now?

Ajit: I knew it. I'm a "one-hit wonder." I'll never top the six prizes, and my father will always look at me like I'm a disappointment.

Once the client has fully activated an underlying belief, the therapist can use one of several approaches to restructuring the early memory. For example, the therapist can encourage the client to take the perspective of the person delivering the painful message by asking the client to play the role of that person while the therapist plays the role of the client at the time of the key life event. Ajit's therapist used this approach so that he could begin to consider reasons why his father would respond to him in the manner he did. The dialogue takes place after Ajit agreed to play the role of his father. In this role-play, Ajit played the role of his father, and his therapist played the role of Ajit in fifth grade after the awards ceremony.

> *Therapist:* But, Father, I still won two prizes. In fact, I've won prizes every year. I'm proud of myself.
>
> *Ajit:* It doesn't matter. Last year was fourth grade; this year is fifth grade. You're going backward rather than forward.
>
> *Therapist:* OK, Father, I understand that I won fewer prizes this year. But, maybe it doesn't mean that I'm moving backward. Maybe there is a different reason. Maybe some of the other kids have finally started to study like I do. Or maybe the teachers don't want to give me all of the prizes so that the other kids don't get discouraged.
>
> *Ajit:* Son, trust me on this, you need to keep pushing ahead. Our country has faced hard economic times. I came from nothing. You don't want to find yourself in the same position as my father, who could barely feed his family.
>
> *Therapist:* Ajit, let's jump out of the role-play for a moment. What are you learning about your father's response to you?
>
> *Ajit:* I think he was a stoic man who thought it was weak to praise his child, especially your oldest son, for a job well done.
>
> *Therapist:* Was that sort of fathering typical for the time and culture in which you grew up?
>
> *Ajit:* Yes, especially among successful men at the top of their career. [pauses] But there's something else. My father came from very little. He remembers what it was like not to have enough food and to wear torn clothes, or clothes that were too small.
>
> *Therapist:* Ah, so what does that suggest about the motivation behind his comments toward you?
>
> *Ajit:* Maybe it was *his* way of showing that he cares. That he didn't want me to live a hard life.
>
> *Therapist:* If the old way of viewing your father's reaction to you is that he's disappointed in you, the new way would be what?

Ajit: He didn't feel that he could afford to be proud of me. That he needed to do everything he could to ensure that I was successful so that my life, and even my children's lives, were not as hard as his was when he was growing up.

Therapist: Do you still believe fully that your father was disappointed in you?

Ajit: No, maybe not disappointed. Wanting the best for me, but not understanding that his interpersonal styles did a lot of damage.

Another way to use role-play to restructure early memories is to have clients play the role of their younger selves during a key life event and prompting these clients to respond from the perspective of their present selves using the cognitive restructuring tools that they have acquired. Consider this dialogue with Ajit.

Therapist: Fifth-grade Ajit, I'd like to have your older self, at your present age, enter into this dialogue and provide perspective. Is that OK?

Ajit: Yes.

Therapist: Fifth-grade Ajit, tell older Ajit how you feel.

Ajit: I'm sad. I'm really down on myself. My father is disappointed in me for winning only two of six possible prizes. I'm a loser.

Therapist: How does your older self answer back?

Ajit: He's not disappointed. And you are *not* a loser. This is just the way he is. He remembers back when the region of India in which he grew up was in economic crisis. He just wants to make sure that you do everything you can to be successful.

Therapist: What does fifth-grade Ajit say?

Ajit: But he's still right, in a way. What if I really am a "one-hit wonder?"

Therapist: Older Ajit?

Ajit: There's no way you'll be a "one-hit wonder." You keep earning prizes, even if you don't win all six of them. That shows that you are still one of the top students in the school.

Therapist: Fifth-grade Ajit, do you buy this?

Ajit: Sort of. But it seems like Father is never happy with me. I'm always scared to show him my grades. I really do think he looks at me like I'm inadequate.

[Therapist is about to jump in and ask older Ajit to respond, but Ajit says, "I got this."]

Ajit: His response to you has more to do with his personality and his generation than it does you. No one in the history of the school had ever won six prizes, and to my knowledge, no one ever has since then. It might be impossible for *anyone* to keep up that level of performance. But history showed that you continued to perform at the top level the entire time you were in school. And beyond.

Therapist: What wonderful work, Ajit. It's a real tribute to great thought that you have put into our work together. Let's jump out of the role-play now. When we first started to examine this belief of being a "one-hit wonder," you believed it at a level of 95%. Now how much do you believe it?

Ajit: I really don't believe it anymore. That's not to say that I have eliminated the stress and anxiety associated with running my own business. I clearly need to continue to work on ways to manage my stress. But this core belief of being a "one-hit wonder?" It simply isn't true.

IMAGERY RESCRIPTING

Imagery rescripting is a powerful belief modification technique that helps clients to (a) transform negative images that form the basis of underlying beliefs into more benign images; and (b) create new, positive images that contain key elements that support a new, healthier belief (Holmes, Arntz, & Smucker, 2007; Young et al., 2003). The rationale for this technique is that imagery is thought to be associated with much more powerful emotional reactions than verbal processing of the same content (Holmes et al., 2007); thus, it stands to reason that modification of key images that keep unhelpful core beliefs entrenched would provide the context for substantial belief modification. Shane, for example, carried with him an image of walking home from a pizza restaurant alone with his head hanging after his high school girlfriend ended the relationship. Through the use of imagery rescripting, Shane could construct an alternative image, such as walking with his head held high into the sunset, readying himself for the next phase of his life in college, where he would be sure to meet many young women with whom he would be interested in beginning a relationship. His mental image, then, would be transformed from one representing undesirability and an associated sense of shame to one representing optimism and possibility.

Conclusion

Core beliefs are fundamental beliefs that people hold about themselves, others, and the way the world works, whereas intermediate beliefs are the rules and assumptions by which we live our lives that stem from underlying core beliefs. Although many clients receive great benefit from strategies such as cognitive restructuring of automatic thoughts, behavioral activation, and problem solving, others find that they achieve the greatest change from CBT when they shift old, unhelpful underlying beliefs to new beliefs that are healthier and more balanced. In this chapter, we described a small number of belief modification techniques, including ways to identify underlying beliefs, ways to define new beliefs, the implementation of behavior changes to reinforce new belief, the use of the positive data log, the use of the cognitive continuum, historical testing of unhelpful beliefs, the restructuring of early memories, and imagery rescripting. In reality, there is an array of belief modification techniques, and cognitive behavioral therapists need not be limited to the techniques described in this chapter. We encourage the interested reader to consult additional resources, including J. S. Beck (2011), D. Dobson and Dobson (2009), Hays (2014), Persons et al. (2001), and Wenzel (2012). Recent work by Robert Leahy (2015) on emotional schemas also suggests new and exciting ways to conceptualize and practice belief change in CBT.

We are often asked by novice cognitive behavioral therapists, "What should we work on first—automatic thoughts or underlying beliefs?" There is no answer to this question that is always correct; every client is different, is at a different stage of preparedness for change, and has different preferences. The choice of intervention should be guided by a collaborative consideration of the case conceptualization. This being said, in most instances, we recommend that cognitive behavioral therapists begin with a focus on the "here-and-now" with their clients and use strategies that are meant to bring about fairly immediate changes in clients' life circumstances. These interventions often include behavioral activation, problem solving, and cognitive restructuring of automatic thoughts. The restructuring of underlying beliefs tends to take time, which stretches across the course of many sessions; thus, when clients have basic CBT tools in place, they will usually have had practice with using these tools to solve problems or to feel better, which should, in turn, allow them space to work systematically on addressing underlying beliefs. However, if a client has a strong preference for working in the early sessions on belief modification, then the therapist usually complies, especially if the client has previous experience with CBT.

It should be acknowledged that scholarly discourse on strategies to shift unhelpful core beliefs is in its infancy, and there is limited research that has examined the degree to which the implementation of belief modification techniques is associated with change above and beyond the techniques described in the volume to this point. We are eager for research to address this empirical question. In the meantime, we encourage cognitive behavioral therapists to function as scientist-practitioners, collecting data from clients as treatment proceeds to evaluate the degree to which these belief modification techniques (or any cognitive behavioral techniques, for that matter) are exerting their desired effects and resulting in decreased symptomatology, increased skillfulness, or increased quality of life.

Relapse Prevention and the Completion of Treatment

6

A fundamental tenet of cognitive behavioral therapy (CBT) is that clients acquire skills and knowledge that they can eventually apply on their own, without the need for a therapist. Thus, cognitive behavioral therapists encourage clients to recognize cognitive and behavioral principles of change throughout treatment so that they can recognize and implement these principles in their own lives outside of session, and then generalize the knowledge and skills that they have acquired to other challenges and stressors that were not the direct focus in session. When clients achieve this consolidation of learning, they are likely ready to move toward the end of treatment.

Exhibit 6.1 summarizes signs that indicate that it is time to move into the late phase of treatment. Recall that cognitive behavioral therapists collect objective data about the severity of key symptoms during the brief mood check. One heuristic used by many cognitive behavioral therapists is to raise the possibility of moving into the late phase of treatment with the client when he or she has scored in the minimal to mild

http://dx.doi.org/10.1037/14936-007
Cognitive Behavioral Therapy Techniques and Strategies, by A. Wenzel, K. S. Dobson, and P. A. Hays

EXHIBIT 6.1

Signs That a Client Is Ready for the Late Phase of Treatment

- Client's objective ratings of depression, anxiety, and/or other symptoms gathered from each session's brief mood check fall in the minimal to mild range for at least three consecutive sessions.
- Client no longer meets diagnostic criteria for the mental health disorder that brought him or her into treatment.
- Client has solved the problems that brought him or her into treatment.
- Client has completed homework and has observed positive changes in his or her life as a result.
- Treatment goals have been met.

range of symptomatology for at least three consecutive sessions. If therapists use a 0-to-10 Likert-type scale to assess key symptoms of a client's clinical presentation, then the mild range might be defined as a 3 or lower. If therapists administer self-report inventories of symptoms, such as the Beck Depression Inventory—II (A. T. Beck, Steer, & Brown, 1996), then they can use the scoring guidelines associated with those instruments to determine when a client has moved into the minimal to mild range.

The ratings obtained during the brief mood check are only one source of information that cognitive behavioral therapists use to determine when it is appropriate to move into the late phase of treatment. Therapists also consider whether clients continue to meet diagnostic criteria for the mental health disorder with which they presented for treatment; whether the problems that brought them to treatment have been solved; the degree to which the client have completed homework; the degree to which the completion of homework has translated to positive life changes; and the extent to which treatment goals have been met. We encourage cognitive behavioral therapists to consider multiple outcome indices to guide movement into the late phase of treatment. There will be many cases in which a client rates the severity of symptoms as more than mild but nevertheless reports a significant reduction in symptoms, demonstrates the ability to apply cognitive and behavioral tools in his or her life, and has met treatment goals. It would likely be appropriate for this client to move into the late phase of treatment. We note that the movement into the late phase of treatment is not determined unilaterally by the cognitive behavioral therapist, but rather, it is ideally agreed on after careful consideration of all of these pieces of information by the therapist and client together.

This chapter describes the typical activities in which therapists and clients engage in the late phase of treatment, including the development of a relapse prevention plan, the consolidation of learning, tapering sessions, and addressing any negative reactions associated with the completion of treatment. In addition, it illustrates the progress made by the three clients described in this book, Shane, Beth, and Ajit, and the manner in which their therapists approached the late phase of treatment with them.

Relapse Prevention

Relapse prevention is a strategy for clients to use their new knowledge and skills to prevent a relapse or a recurrence of the problems that brought them into treatment. *Relapse* is defined as an exacerbation of symptoms before the episode of the mental health disorder has remitted, whereas *recurrence* is a new episode of a mental health disorder that emerges after remission has been achieved. Cognitive behavioral therapists who implement relapse prevention typically encourage their clients to identify (a) warning signs that signal the possibility of a relapse or a recurrence, (b) tools that they can use to cope with and address their symptoms and problems, (c) people in their social support network who they can contact for support or help, (d) indicators that they should contact a professional for help, and (e) contact information for professional help. This information can be assimilated into a written *relapse prevention plan* that clients can store in a safe place and consult as needed. Figure 6.1 is an example of the relapse prevention plan that Ajit created in consultation with his therapist.

A unique series of exercises that is implemented in the cognitive behavioral treatment of suicidal patients involves the use of vivid imagery to recreate the circumstances that brought the client to treatment and to rehearse the manner in which cognitive and behavioral tools could be applied to manage those circumstances, as well as future circumstances that have the potential to be challenging or stressful (Wenzel, Brown, & Beck, 2009). This *relapse prevention protocol* is typically administered across at least two sessions in the late phase of treatment. Its purpose is to provide clear and compelling evidence to both the client and therapist that the client has acquired and can apply an array of cognitive and behavioral tools to manage emotional distress and solve problems. Exhibit 6.2 lists the main features of the relapse prevention protocol.

Cognitive behavioral therapists take care to explain the protocol and its rationale in detail, answering any questions and addressing any concerns that the client might have. They ensure that their client understands and concurs with the purpose of the exercises, and they obtain their client's consent to proceed. Next, they engage in the first of three imaginal exercises, which is to visualize and describe, in detail, the events that led to the client's decision to seek treatment. During these imaginal exercises, clients close their eyes if they are comfortable doing

FIGURE 6.1

RELAPSE PREVENTION PLAN	
Warning signs: *How do I know that I need to use the information on my relapse prevention plan?*	• Looking at myself like a "one-hit wonder" • Increased conflict with employees • Disrupted sleep schedule • Not taking care of myself (e.g., excessive drinking, not eating well, no exercise)
Coping tools: *How can I apply what I learned in CBT?*	• Complete a thought record. • Read my coping cards. • Do a nonwork activity that makes me feel good (e.g., running, rowing, photography)
Social support: *Who can I contact for support and help?*	• My sister • My mother • My friend Kai
Indications that I should call a professional: *How do I know that it is time to reach out for professional help?*	• Hopelessness • Making bad choices even though I know I should take care of myself • Volatility in the work place
Professional contacts:	• My therapist (222.222.2222) • My psychiatrist (333.333.3333)

Completed relapse prevention plan.

so, and they speak in the present tense, as if the events were occurring in the present moment. The therapist prompts the client to supply details to enhance the imaginal experience, especially details that involve the five senses. Clients who engage in this exercise often learn that they can tolerate emotional distress without engaging in self-defeating behavior. In the second and third imaginal rehearsal exercises, the therapist prompts the client to describe the manner in which he or she would apply specific cognitive and behavioral tools. Imaginal rehearsal increases the likelihood that clients will apply cognitive and behavioral tools in their own lives outside of session. Clients who engage in these exercises develop confidence that they will be able to handle crises and stressors in the future, after they have completed treatment.

EXHIBIT 6.2

Relapse Prevention Protocol

▪ Orient client to the rationale underlying the relapse prevention protocol and the manner in which it will proceed, and obtain client's consent to move forward.
▪ Ask the client to imagine, in detail, the events that led to the decision to seek treatment.
▪ Ask the client to imagine, in detail, the manner in which he or she would apply cognitive and behavioral tools to manage emotional distress associated with the events that led to the decision to seek treatment.
▪ Ask the client to imagine, in detail, a reasonable future stressor or crisis and the manner in which he or she would apply cognitive and behavioral tools to manage associated emotional distress.
▪ Thoroughly debrief the client, including (a) assessing for and addressing any residual emotional distress from the exercise, and (b) encouraging the client to articulate what he or she learned from participating in the exercise.

Shane's therapist implemented the relapse prevention protocol with him in the late phase of treatment. Recall that, at the time of his first session, Shane reported that he was in crisis and requested that he and his therapist focus on the acquisition of skills to manage his emotional distress, rather than on diagnosis and assessment. Thus, in this phase of the relapse prevention protocol, Shane's therapist prompted him to imagine the events that led to his crisis and describe the way in which he would apply the cognitive and behavioral tools that he had acquired throughout the course of treatment.

> *Therapist:* I'd like you to close your eyes and again describe the events that led to the crisis that you were experiencing when I first met you, as if they were happening again. But this time, you will imagine using the tools that you have learned in treatment and the effects that the use of those tools have on your emotional distress. Is this something that you are willing to do?
>
> [Shane nods his head, closes his eyes, and sinks back into the couch.]
>
> *Therapist:* You can begin whenever you are ready.
>
> *Shane:* I'm in my apartment all alone. It's a big football weekend, playoffs. Everyone seems to be going to a party or to a sports bar. But nobody has invited me.

Therapist: What is running through your mind right now?

Shane: That no one wants me. That maybe I shouldn't even stick around if this is the way things will be.

Therapist: And what are you feeling emotionally?

Shane: Down. Just really, really down. But also antsy at the same time. I'm bored, I don't know what to do. I can't quiet my mind.

Therapist: What are you thinking of doing about that?

Shane: I should just drink. Take a few shots. Numb myself out. [laughs sarcastically] Who knows, maybe drinking will help me to get up the guts to end it all.

Therapist: Are you having thoughts of hurting yourself?

Shane: [quietly] Yeah, I am.

Therapist: Think back to what you have learned from our work together. How could you use this learning to get you through this emerging crisis?

Shane: Well, I know drinking just makes it worse. I need to do something else.

Therapist: What activities, specifically, have we identified in our work together?

Shane: I could call my mom or dad, maybe even go there to visit. I could go for a run. That always makes me feel better; it's kind of like a release.

Therapist: What do you decide to do?

Shane: I'll go for a run. The cold air will feel good, maybe shake me out of this funk.

Therapist: How far do you run?

Shane: Umm, 3 miles. Just enough to feel good.

Therapist: How does it feel to be outdoors running?

Shane: I feel the cold air on my face. It feels different than my hot, stuffy apartment. And it's sunny out, even though it's cold, and there is snow on the ground. So I can feel some warmth on my face.

Therapist: Imagine that you are back inside after completing the run. How do you feel?

Shane: Better, actually.

Therapist: Before the run, you had said that you felt really down, antsy, and bored. Are you continuing to have these emotional experiences?

Shane: No, not exactly. Well, maybe I'm still down. But it's not as bad.

Therapist: What's running through your mind right now?

Shane: I don't really think anything is running through my mind.

Therapist: Before the run, you said that it might not be worth it to stick around if this is the way things will be and that you had thoughts of hurting yourself. Where do you stand on these kinds of thoughts now?

Shane: [sighs] I'm not focused on them anymore. But, I'm not gonna lie to you, they're still in the back of my mind.

Therapist: I appreciate your honesty, Shane. What would be a longer term strategy that you can use to address this sense of hopelessness?

Shane: [thinking for a moment] Well, I really like that list of all of the people in my life who are close to me or who have been close to me in the past. I can look at that list again.

Therapist: Imagine that you're looking at that list. What occurs to you?

Shane: That I'd really be hurting a lot of people if I commit suicide. And, just because I'm alone in my apartment, it doesn't mean that I'm truly all alone in my life.

Therapist: Shane, let's jump out of the role-play for a moment. [Shane opens his eyes and sits up straight.] What did you learn from participating in this exercise?

Shane: That that night could have gone a whole lot differently. I cut myself really deep after having five shots. I was almost delirious. I still have a scar from it.

Therapist: And what if you were to experience a similar type of episode in the future?

Shane: I don't think I will. I have a girlfriend now. Everything is so much better!

Therapist: Yes, I'm so pleased that things in your life have turned around. It's a real tribute to the fact that you stuck with CBT, even if you were skeptical at first. [pauses] But would you be willing to humor me for a moment?

Shane: [smiles] OK.

Therapist: Disappointments are inevitable in life. If you were to experience a disappointment that was associated with that sense of being very down, antsy, and bored—perhaps even hopeless—how confident are you that you could use what you have learned in treatment and thwart urges to do something self-destructive?

Shane: I'm very confident. Like a 9 or 10 out of 10. Doing this exercise showed me that these feelings are temporary, even if they don't seem like it in the moment. Like you said, if I can just ride the wave and do something healthy, like running or reaching out to my parents, then the wave goes down again.

Therapist: [setting up the context for another relapse prevention exercise] I wonder if it would be useful to imagine a disappointment or crisis that you might face in the future, and you can, again, walk through the way in which you would apply the tools you acquired in treatment.

Shane: I guess so.

Therapist: What scenario, specifically, would be quite a challenge for you in the future?

Shane: [trembling] I *really* hate to think about it. It would be my girlfriend breaking up with me. I really do think it is going to work out. But I guess I should be prepared in case it doesn't.

After each imaginal exercise, cognitive behavioral therapists do a thorough debriefing with clients. To further consolidate learning, they ask their clients what they learned from the exercise and ways they can apply that knowledge when faced with future stressors or challenges. They also assess for any residual negative affect or agitation. It is our experience that most clients respond to this intervention and view it as an important learning experience. However, in the event that a client has a negative reaction, therapists can take many courses of action. For example, they can lead the client through a breathing or relaxation exercise. They can apply cognitive restructuring to reframe any unhelpful automatic thoughts about the effects of participating in the exercise. They can develop a plan with the client to use the client's social support system or engage in pleasurable or soothing activities. They can also check in with the client between sessions or schedule a subsequent session sooner than they would have otherwise to monitor the client's negative affect and ability to cope.

Although this relapse prevention protocol was developed specifically for inclusion in a CBT package geared toward suicide prevention, it is not difficult to see that imaginal rehearsal can facilitate the consolidation of learning and planning for the ending of treatment with most clients. Thus, cognitive behavioral therapists can adapt this series of exercises to have many clients gain practice with tolerating and coping with emotional distress, as well as demonstrating the way in which they would tolerate and cope with future challenges.

Ending Treatment

It is typical for clients who attend regular therapy sessions (e.g., weekly or biweekly) to taper to a reduced frequency as they begin to improve. Such spacing of sessions allows clients to achieve greater independence and apply cognitive and behavioral tools on their own to resolve life problems in their lives. Some clients also schedule *booster sessions* after the completion of treatment to check in with their therapist, provide an update on successes and challenges, and "brush up" on any aspect of their cognitive behavioral work that they might have forgotten. These sessions can be held 3 or 6 months after the completion of treatment or after any amount of time that the client believes is appropriate.

There is no precise heuristic to follow when deciding when and how to taper sessions and schedule booster sessions; such decisions are made on the basis of the cognitive case conceptualization and in collaboration with the client. Shane, for example, attended 50 sessions throughout the course of 15 months. During the first 3 months of treatment, he attended two sessions per week; once he reported a stable decrease in suicidal ideation and hopelessness, he attended one session per week; and in the last 2 months of treatment, he attended sessions on a biweekly basis. He chose not to schedule a booster session, claiming that wanted to "put that part of my life behind me and look toward the future." Beth attended 20 weekly sessions of CBT across 7 months. She scheduled three booster sessions, each 4 to 6 weeks apart from one another, and she then ended treatment. Ajit attended 12 sessions of CBT across the course of 6 months. His attendance was a bit sporadic and was determined, in large part, by his availability, as he had a great deal of business travel and obligations with his clients. In his final session, he chose not to schedule a booster session because he was unsure of his schedule 3 or 6 months in the future, but he requested the option of maintaining e-mail and telephone contact with his therapist so that he could schedule as needed.

The knowledge and tools that clients acquire in CBT are meant to last a lifetime. However, to ensure that such knowledge and tools are accessible when they are needed, clients need to continue to use and practice them in their lives. This does not mean that clients must keep written homework as if they were regularly attending sessions. However, it does mean that clients will ideally be aware of cognitive and behavioral principles as they face their life problems and that they will implement the tools when it is appropriate to do so. Many clients go back to more "formal" cognitive behavioral exercises (e.g., completing a thought record, reviewing a coping card) in particularly challenging situations. In addition, clients can schedule periodic *self-sessions* (J. S. Beck, 2011; D. Dobson & Dobson, 2009) in which they devote time to (a) identifying life problems or areas of emotional well-being that need attention, (b) reviewing their notes and handouts from their previous course of CBT, (c) applying cognitive behavioral principles and tools to move toward resolving any issues, and (d) committing to more systematic implementation of these principles and tools in their lives.

It is our experience that the majority of clients who undergo a full course of CBT feel good about their progress at the end of treatment and report confidence that they can apply the principles and tools in their lives once therapy has ended. However, there is a subset of clients who, despite having a relapse prevention plan in place, report anxiety or sadness about the end of treatment. After all, they have likely developed a strong relationship with their therapist that is characterized by mutual warmth and respect. They likely have also come to appreciate therapy appointments as a safe place to discuss their feelings and address problems that they might not like to admit to others. In the late phase of treatment, cognitive behavioral therapists assess for unhelpful automatic thoughts and emotional distress associated with the ending of treatment, and they use cognitive restructuring to bring balance and perspective to their attitude toward ending treatment. Consider this dialogue with Beth, who struggled with the end of treatment despite the fact that she recognized significant gains and no longer met criteria for a mental health disorder.

> *Beth:* [tearful] I'm sorry. I know I shouldn't be this upset. Right from the beginning, we talked about the fact that there is an ending to treatment.

> *Therapist:* [handing Beth a tissue and normalizing her reactions] Beth, plenty of my clients experience emotional upset when they are face to face with the end of treatment. That goes for therapists, too. I'll certainly miss seeing you on a regular basis. It's been gratifying for me to see that CBT has made such a difference in your life.

> *Beth:* I know, I know. I truly believe that I've made a lot of progress as well. But . . . but I don't know, who will I talk to if I'm struggling again?

Therapist: I wonder if there's an automatic thought there. If I find myself struggling again, then . . . what?

Beth: [crying] Then I'll have no one to talk to, and it will get worse, and I will go right back to where I started.

Therapist: It's a good thing that you know how to answer thoughts like that. What is a more balanced way of viewing this situation?

Beth: [blowing her nose] I guess it's not like I have no one to talk to. I've made friends with another one of the teachers, and she feels the same way I do.

Therapist: And how do you respond to the idea that you'll get worse, and that you'll go right back to where you started?

Beth: Well, it's not automatic that I will get worse. I can always turn to my relapse prevention plan and use the skills that I've learned in here. [Therapist nods.] And, I guess being upset about something doesn't have to mean that I'm going to have another episode of full-fledged depression, right?

Therapist: Exactly. I couldn't have said it better myself. It is very true that ups and downs are a normal part of life. So feeling down, anxious, upset, or any other negative emotion is not the equivalent of having a recurrence of depression and anxiety. And you are equipped with tools to catch these emotional experiences early on and do something skillful to address them well before they turn into a mental health disorder. [pauses] How much do you believe that?

Beth: That everyone has ups and downs? And that downs don't have to be full-fledged depression?

Therapist: Yes.

Beth: I do, I believe it 100%. I just have to remember that in the moment. Maybe I should add that to my relapse prevention plan?

Therapist: I think that would be a terrific idea.

Notice that Beth's therapist took the opportunity to normalize the emotional "ups and downs" that most people experience in daily living. Some clients hold the mistaken belief that *any* upsetting emotional experience signifies a return of a mental health problem. As a result, they might avoid emotional experiences, or they might be vigilant for indicators of emotional upset, to the point that they interfere with their quality of life.

Clients can be taught that normal fluctuations in mood are different from the warning signs that indicate the possible relapse or a recurrence of a mental health disorder, as identified in the relapse prevention plan. It is hoped that this normalization facilitates the acceptance of fluctuations in mood and detachment of significance or meaning attributed to them.

Conclusion

Clients enter the late phase of treatment when there is evidence that they have made significant and sustained progress. There are many sources of this evidence, including decreases in ratings made during the brief mood check, decreases in symptoms associated with mental health disorder diagnoses, the solution of problems that clients had at the beginning of treatment, the successful completion of homework over the course of several settings, and the meeting of treatment goals. The goals of the late phase of treatment are to (a) summarize gains made in treatment using relapse prevention techniques, such as the development of a relapse prevention plan or participation in imaginal relapse prevention exercises; (b) taper and then end sessions; and (c) address any upsetting cognitive and emotional reactions to the ending of treatment. The activities in the late phase of treatment solidify the clients' confidence that they can apply their skills and knowledge to manage future stressors, challenges, and disappointments.

Some clients who successfully complete a course of CBT will contact their therapist in the future to resume treatment. From a relapse prevention perspective, it is adaptive for clients to reach out and contact their therapist when they notice warning signs that do not seem to be tempered by the self-administration of cognitive and behavioral tools. In almost all cases, when clients return to treatment, they do not start from "square one." Instead, they simply require a "tune-up" through a few booster sessions, or some extra support as they go through a challenging life experience. Our stance is that cognitive behavioral therapists, and mental health systems in general, would do well to adopt the idea of an "open door" for treatment and an attitude that facilitation of quick response to care is much better than emphasizing the need for clear "termination" in therapy; a return to treatment should not be viewed as a failure (O'Donohue & Cucciare, 2008).

Culturally Responsive Cognitive Behavioral Therapy 7

magine that you have 1 minute to describe yourself by completing the statement "I am . . ." Your finished sentence might identify you as Latina, middle class, Jewish, a student, a parent of a disabled child, divorced, Japanese, a woman, White, gay, bilingual, transgender, or other aspects of your identity. It is likely that you have many ways to identify yourself because we human beings are complex. At the same time, we often perceive others more simplistically, focusing on a particular characteristic that distinguishes an individual from the majority or from ourselves. Furthermore, we often assume that this one characteristic tells us what the person believes, thinks, feels, and does. Nothing could be further from the truth.

Research shows that there is as much diversity within groups as there is between groups. For this and several other reasons, the influence of culture can be complicated to understand, especially with respect to the therapeutic relationship. As therapists, we need to consider the cultural influences on our clients and also on ourselves. Culture shapes what we

http://dx.doi.org/10.1037/14936-008
Cognitive Behavioral Therapy Techniques and Strategies, by A. Wenzel, K. S. Dobson, and P. A. Hays

think, feel, and do, so the more we understand these influences, the more able we will be to form caring, respectful relationships; formulate useful hypotheses; ask relevant questions; and implement interventions that help our clients.

This chapter begins with an outline of several ways in which cognitive behavioral therapy (CBT) is especially useful in multicultural situations. Attention is then given to CBT's limitations, followed by suggestions for making CBT more culturally responsive. Throughout the information provided, the focus is on nine cultural influences highlighted by the ADDRESSING framework: Age and generational influences, Developmental or other Disability, Religion and spiritual orientation, Ethnic and racial identity, Socioeconomic status, Sexual orientation, Indigenous heritage, National origin, and Gender (see Table 7.1; Hays, 2016). These are not the only cultural influences that can affect psycho-

TABLE 7.1

ADDRESSING Cultural Influences

Cultural influences	Dominant group	Nondominant/minority
Age and generational influences	Young/middle-age adults	Children, older adults
Developmental or other Disability	Nondisabled people	People with cognitive, intellectual, sensory, physical, and/or psychiatric disability
Religion and spirituality	Christian and secular	Muslims, Jews, Hindus, Buddhists, and other religions
Ethnic and racial identity	European Americans	Asian, South Asian, Latino, Pacific Islander, African, Arab, African American, Middle Eastern, and multiracial people
Socioeconomic status	Upper and middle class	People of lower status by occupation, education, income, or inner-city/rural habitat
Sexual orientation	Heterosexuals	People who identify as gay, lesbian, or bisexual
Indigenous heritage	European Americans	American Indians, Inuit, Alaska Natives, Métis, Native Hawaiians, New Zealand Māori, and Aboriginal Australians
National origin	U.S.-born Americans	Immigrants, refugees, and international students
Gender	Men	Women and people who identify as transgender

Note. Adapted from *Addressing Cultural Complexities in Practice: Assessment, Diagnosis, and Therapy, Third Edition* (p. 8), by P. A. Hays, 2016, Washington, DC: American Psychological Association. Copyright 2016 by the American Psychological Association.

therapy; however, they are ones that have been noted by the American Psychological Association (2003) and the American Counseling Association (Arredondo & Pérez, 2006) to require special attention because of their historical neglect.

CBT and Multicultural Practice

Recent research supports the cultural adaptation of CBT, particularly with members of ethnic minority cultures. When taken together, the results of three meta-analyses have found that adaptations were helpful, and the more specific the therapy is to the culture, the more effective psychotherapy was for primary outcome measures of psychological functioning in psychotic, mood, and other behavioral disorders (Benish, Quintana, & Wampold, 2011; Huey, Tilley, Jones, & Smith, 2014; Smith, Rodríguez, & Bernal, 2011).

CBT is particularly well suited for multicultural work in at least five ways. First, CBT emphasizes the need to conduct case conceptualization and to tailor interventions to each client's unique situation, and this position counters stereotypical thinking regarding members of minority identities. Second, CBT emphasizes clients' expertise regarding themselves and their ability to learn and apply skills in the future without the need for a therapist. This emphasis communicates respect, and respect is a key value held by members of many minority cultures. Third, CBT emphasizes conscious processes that can be described and taught. This approach is particularly important with clients who are less verbal or who have limited language proficiency and with individuals who come from cultures where the unconscious is not a commonly understood concept. Fourth, CBT focuses on a holistic understanding of clients including cultural strengths and supports that can be used to reinforce desired change. This recognition of culturally based resilience factors is also empowering and shows respect. Fifth, CBT is firmly rooted in behaviorism, which focuses on the influence of environments on behavior. Culture is a foundational part of social and physical environments and as such can be incorporated into CBT.

At the same time, there are some limitations to CBT's multicultural applications. First, although an individual's personal history is important, CBT has typically focused on the individual—to the neglect of cultural influences—and on the present over the past. These tendencies may lead an inexperienced therapist to overlook relevant historical and present-day influences on the client's health and behavior. Second, although CBT is relatively holistic in its consideration of emotions, physical sensations, behavior, cognition, and the environment, research on CBT has historically neglected spirituality and religion. Third, with its reliance on quantifiable measures, CBT is often assumed to be a value-neutral approach. However, CBT and most of the major psychotherapies are clearly biased toward personal characteristics and behaviors most valued in the dominant culture, such as individual independence (over interdependence), assertiveness (over subtle communication and harmony), talking (over listening and observing), change (over acceptance), and rational cognition (over a less linear worldview; Hays, 2009).

The Therapist's Personal Work

Culturally responsive practice begins with the therapist's personal work, including recognition of personal biases and ongoing work to change these biases by actively seeking out new experiences, research, introspection, and consultation. This work also includes consideration of the ways in which personal identities bring privilege that can limit understanding of clients who do not have such privilege.

As therapists, it is especially important to know our areas of bias and privilege because privilege tends to cut off those who have it from information about and a deeper understanding of those who do not. For example, when working with a gay Asian American client, a White male heterosexual therapist will not—indeed, cannot—have the depth of experience regarding how it is to be a gay man of color, nor is he likely to have the same easy access to such information as would a gay therapist of color. Although this does not mean that the White therapist cannot develop a good understanding and connection with the client, such a connection will probably require more work on his part.

Perceiving one's own biases and privilege is difficult because, as the saying goes, privilege is like oxygen: You don't know it's there until it's gone. One way to begin this process is to begin examining cultural influences that have affected your own beliefs, behaviors, relationships, and worldview. This consideration involves asking how your Age and the generational influences on you (including experiences related to your age cohort, and generational roles such as being a parent or oldest son or daughter) have shaped your beliefs, behaviors, and relationships; how your experience with disability (e.g., a Developmental disability, or other Disability) has shaped your experiences, opportunities, and behavior; how Religious or spiritual beliefs have shaped your worldview, and how Ethnic and racial identity, Socioeconomic status, Sexual orientation, Indigenous heritage, National origin, and Gender (i.e., the ADDRESSING influences) have influenced you. This exploration is an ongoing process that expands with increasing exposure to and interaction with people of diverse identities (Hays, 2013).

The Therapeutic Alliance

Across different theoretical orientations, several common factors clearly contribute to treatment outcome. It has been suggested that the therapeutic relationship accounts for 30% of the outcome variance, and that 40% is due to external factors including clients themselves, 15% can be attributed to client expectations, and 15% to specific theory and treatment techniques (Norcross & Lambert, 2011). Multicultural situations pose a challenge for the formation of a positive therapeutic alliance due to the range of social norms that govern relationships. A good starting point is to begin learning a diversity of behaviors that demonstrate respect in different cultures because respect is a central value in Latino, Asian, Native, Middle Eastern, African, and African American cultures.

Of course, the specific behaviors that demonstrate respect vary between and within cultures. For example, many Latino people expect a warmer, more personal interaction before doing business, whereas many Arab people expect a cordial but more formal approach. However, *within* Latino cultures, some elders may expect a more formal interaction, and *within* Arab cultures, women meeting alone with a female therapist may prefer a less formal approach.

As you learn about diverse respect behaviors, we recommend a hypothesis-testing approach to initial interactions. This involves paying attention to emotional cues in both the client and yourself, and when you notice that something is "off" or that you are not connecting, asking yourself whether the disconnection may be due to a difference related to age/generational influences, disability, religion, ethnicity, race, or other factors. The more you learn about diverse behaviors, the wider repertoire of hypotheses and alternative behaviors you will have to choose from when you sense that what you're doing is not working.

Thinking Holistically and Systemically

CBT's individualistic, present orientation can be balanced out by a consideration of culture in relation to the five CBT components (i.e., environment, cognition, behavior, emotion, and physical sensations/symptoms).

Environmental considerations include present and historical influences on culture that may affect clients and/or those around them. For example, previous generations' experiences of war, genocide, migration, and systemic oppression may be passed down intergenerationally, resulting in secondary trauma, but also in the development of resilience qualities and skills. Such knowledge regarding clients' cultural histories serves as a mental template within which an individual's personal history makes more sense. It also brings a deeper, more nuanced understanding of the individual and facilitates more accurate hypotheses, relevant questions, nonoffensive language, and the therapeutic alliance.

Although information regarding the client's personal history usually comes from the client, it is unfair to expect clients to educate therapists about their culture. In addition, reliance on clients alone for cultural information is risky because such descriptions are likely to hold biases. Clients can provide information on their personal experience of their culture, but it is the therapist's responsibility to seek out the more general, background information regarding clients' cultures and cultural histories. A *genogram* is a graph that uses symbols to visually illustrate an individual's key relationships. Including cultural information on a genogram can facilitate the process of obtaining the personal information and may raise questions for the therapist to obtain additional cultural information later, outside the session.

When considering culture in relation to the second CBT component of *cognition*, a culturally responsive approach includes recognition of the ways in which culture shapes values, beliefs, interpretation of events, views of self and others, and so on. Although some values are universal (e.g., the desire to love and be loved), the priorities assigned to values can vary greatly across cultures. For example, individuals from European American cultures often place a high value on personal independence, which plays out in an emphasis on personal choice, assertiveness, and individual expression. In contrast, many individuals from Indigenous and Asian cultures place a higher value on interdependence, cooperation, and harmonious relationships. This is not to say that each culture values only interdependence or independence; rather, it emphasizes the relative importance of both values.

Cognitive behavioral therapists also consider the key components of behavior, emotions, and physical sensations. A culturally responsive approach to these domains includes consideration of different definitions of normality and abnormality, and different physical, emotional, and behavioral expressions of health and illness. The dominant culture also shapes all of these components, however; because the majority of therapists belong to dominant cultural groups, they are generally more familiar with dominant norms regarding behavioral, emotional, and bodily experiences and expressions.

Distinguishing Environmental From Cognitive Stressors

Cognitive behavioral therapists distinguish between stressors that are primarily due to environmental factors and those due to cognitions regarding situations and events. Although problems often include both components, this distinction can guide the target of interventions. For example, Beth's work situation involved significant environmental stressors including long hours, excessive paperwork, frustrated parents and teachers, and physical risks in working with children with disabilities; furthermore, most of these stressors were beyond her control. At the same time, her thoughts about the challenges included her tendency to catastrophize (e.g., "The other child is going to be seriously hurt, I will be accountable, and I will lose my job"), which contributed to her emotions of horror, anxiety, and dejection, physical symptoms, and behaviors that worked against her long-term goals (i.e., failing to act, crying uncontrollably, and needing to leave the classroom). Recognizing the reality of Beth's external environment, the therapist validated Beth's experience and feelings, but he also helped her to see how changing her internal self-talk, focus, and interpretation of events could help her feel differently.

The distinction between external environmental stressors and internal cognitive stressors is especially important when working with clients of minority identities for whom prejudice and discrimination are a part of daily life. Minority members' experiences and interpretations are frequently discounted by the dominant culture, so the validation of prejudice, discrimination, and other systemic forms of oppression helps to build trust that the therapist really does understand the individual in his or her context. It can also help the therapist to avoid premature cognitive restructuring—that is, moving into thought-change strategies when the environment needs primary attention. For example, if a client shares an experience of discrimination, it would be important to consider environmental interventions, such as talking to a trusted supervisor or filing a grievance, before suggesting that it is the client who needs to change. Focusing on client change without validation or addressing environmental oppression may be interpreted as blaming the client for the racism, heterosexism, able-ism, or other forms of oppression.

Not all external situations are amenable to change, but even in such cases, validation of the client's experience recognizes the reality of oppression. For example, it is important for the therapist to validate a disabled client's feelings and the reality of negative social attitudes and inaccessible facilities and opportunities (Mona, Romesser-Scehnet, Cameron, & Cardenas, 2006). Similarly, if a transgender client experiences anxiety in public places, the therapist can recognize anxiety-inducing obstacles including work and housing discrimination, social ostracism and ridicule, and transgender-identity related violence (Austin & Craig, 2015; Erickson-Schroth, 2014).

It can be a strategic error to move too quickly into questions that challenge the validity of the person's experience. Invalidating questions (e.g., "Are you sure the exclusion was deliberate?") or minimizing the social and physical risks involved (e.g., "Is there any other way to think about this that would decrease your anxiety?") may be perceived as uncaring or naïve, especially if the therapist does not share the client's minority identity (Kelly, 2006). Consider the case of Shane, who attributed his relationship difficulties to rejection from White women who did not want to date a biracial man. If the therapist, a White woman, had responded initially by asking questions that were geared toward explanations other than racism, it is possible that Shane would have emotionally disconnected from her and not returned. However, because she listened attentively, validated his experience, and then focused on what he wanted from the initial session (coping skills), he stayed engaged enough for her to gradually gain his trust. Once a trusting relationship is established, the therapist may then work with the client on cognitions that add to the client's distress.

Behavioral Interventions

There are probably as many ways to adapt behavioral interventions as there are cultures. One way to stay aware of the variety of adaptations is via an acronym that spells the word CLASS, which stands for the five domains of *C*reating a healthy environment; *L*earning something new (e.g., a skill, habit, or information); *A*ssertiveness, conflict resolution, and other communication skills; *S*ocial support; and *S*elf-care activities (physical, emotional, and spiritual; Hays, 2014). The following provides a few examples of adaptations in each of these domains.

Behavioral strategies that *create a healthy environment* include changes in the client's physical and social environment that reinforce desired behavior. To be culturally responsive, this involves considering available options in the client's environment as well as the client's beliefs and values. For example, in a parenting program with Mexican Americans who placed a high value on family relationships, family rewards were considered as important as individual rewards for children's positive behavior (Barker, Cook, & Borrego, 2010). In another parenting program with Chinese immigrant parents, an obstacle in teaching the concept of reinforcement was the belief that "the more you praise them, the more you'll spoil them," so the therapist simply changed the word "praise" to the more acceptable term "encouragement" (A. S. Lau, 2012).

The effectiveness of behavioral interventions that involve *learning a new skill or behavior* can also be enhanced by attention to culture. For example, in teaching a visual imagery exercise to Latino clients, researchers changed the instruction from "Imagine yourself alone in a beautiful place" to "Imagine sharing a moment with a person who makes you feel at peace" (La Roche, D'Angelo, Gualdron, & Leavell, 2006). This adaptation improved the exercise's effectiveness because it incorporated the social orientation of many Latino people.

Knowledge of culture-specific relationship norms is important when teaching *assertiveness, conflict resolution, and other communication skills.* For example, in working with a traditionally oriented Mexican American family whose father periodically exploded in anger that upset him and the family, Organista (2006) used a suggestion from Comas-Díaz and Duncan (1985) to teach the son to preface his suggestions with phrases such as, "With all due respect, Papa . . ." and "Would you permit me to express how I feel about that?" In a similar adaptation with Puerto Rican clients, facilitators emphasized to parents that adolescents' assertiveness skills were not an attempt to disrespect them (Saéz-Santiago, Bernal, Reyes-Rodríguez, & Bonilla-Silva, 2012).

It is important to note that assertiveness and other forms of communication can pose a real danger for some members of minority cultures. Imagine, for example, the case of an individual who is identified as gay or transgender in a social context that is hostile. People of color and members of some religious minorities may be similarly at risk. Respecting clients' knowledge of their own contexts needs to be paramount, together with respect for the judgment about whether it is helpful and safe to use such skills.

Along these lines, *biculturalism* is a helpful concept that can be used to emphasize the advantage of learning multiple skill sets and thus increase the repertoire of skills from which a client can flexibly choose and adapt. Biculturalism has been defined as "a psychological construct that characterizes the degree to which individuals have internalized aspects of two cultures in terms of their identity, behavior, beliefs, attitudes, values, and worldview and can respond functionally to both ethnic and mainstream cultural cues" (Basilio et al., 2014, p. 540). LaFromboise and Rowe (1983) used the concept of biculturalism when they taught American Indian community leaders dominant-culture (European American) communication skills, with an emphasis on respecting the clients' abilities to decide when, where, and how to use those skills. Although this definition applies to ethnic cultures, the idea can extend to nonethnic cultural groups, as in the example of a disabled client who is competent in the disability culture and in the dominant nondisabled world.

The use of *social support* is beneficial in itself and can be used to reinforce desired behaviors. For example, letting clients know that they may invite others into the assessment or therapy sessions can contribute greatly to clients' comfort level, adherence, and progress in treatment. The ideal form of support is that which occurs naturally in the client's culture, such as support provided by extended family and friends (including non–blood-related kin), culture- and group-specific networks, religious organizations, activities that pass down the history of a culture, traditional celebrations and rituals that unite communities, and social and political action groups, particularly for individuals who have been rejected by family members. When culturally embedded supports are available, behavioral interventions can increase clients' use of them because such supports are more likely to be maintained.

The last CLASS category of behavioral interventions consists of *self-care activities*, including physical, emotional, and spiritual self-care. Because poverty disproportionately affects ethnic minority communities and people with disabilities (Macartney, Bishaw, & Fontenot, 2013; McClure, 2011), it is helpful to keep in mind activities that do not require money and are easily accessible. For example, going to the gym may not be an option for individuals who live in communities that do not have one, who must access it via inconvenient and costly public transportation, or who must pay expensive membership fees. Spiritual self-care activities will not necessarily correspond to a formal religious practice. Many urban dwellers identify more with the concept of spirituality than organized religion, and many Native and non-Native people consider being out in nature to be a spiritual experience.

Cognitive Interventions

Cognitive restructuring is sometimes assumed to be confrontational, but in reality, it is more likely that a cognitive behavioral therapist uses cognitive restructuring in a collaborative way. As mentioned previously, this approach to cognitive restructuring is called *collaborative empiricism*, with the collaborative component being especially important in cultures where smooth, harmonious relationships are highly valued. In this section, we provide examples of collaborative adaptations with diverse people.

EVALUATING HELPFULNESS VERSUS VALIDITY

Cognitive restructuring typically involves helping the client to consider the *validity* and *utility* of cognitions (J. S. Beck, 2011). However, when the client is a minority member and the therapist is not, evaluating the validity of a thought or belief can be problematic because thoughts and beliefs are strongly influenced by culture. To know whether a belief is valid or invalid, the therapist needs to know that culture well, and this knowledge can be elusive if you are not a member of the culture yourself.

One form of cognitive restructuring involves asking the client to look for the evidence supporting a belief, and then even if there is some evidence, asking the client to consider the significance, meaning, or consequence of it via questions such as, "OK, so what would it mean if this were true? So what if this does happen? What's the worst that can happen?" Such questions often work well with members of the dominant culture who have more resources and potential supports. In contrast, these questions may be seen as naïve or uncaring when posed to people living in poverty or marginalized communities. For example, if clients lose their job, they or a family member might end up on the streets, back in jail, living in an abusive or violent situation, or without enough food for their children.

An alternative strategy and often a safer approach involves helping clients consider the helpfulness (i.e., utility) of a cognition. Questions might include "How do you feel when you think this? Is it helpful for you to say this thought to yourself, to hold onto this belief, or to focus on this image?" Such questions put clients in the role of expert regarding their own emotions and behavior and can be used as a lead into exploring cognitions that might be more helpful. Of course there will be exceptions, such as when clients use words like *always* or *never* to describe stressors (i.e., demonstrating all-or-nothing thinking), but collaborative examination of the helpfulness of a cognition is often more empowering and avoids inaccurate assumptions about the client's context.

BELIEF WORK

When the therapist judges a core cultural belief to be unhelpful, caution is advised in suggesting the idea of changing it. An initial, careful query may be used to ascertain whether the belief is central to how the client views cultural membership. If the client says that it is central, then it is important not to push on this. Of course, if clients indicate an openness to reconsidering a belief, the therapist may proceed cautiously.

If a client does not wish to consider changing a core cultural belief, it is still possible to engage the individual and work around the belief. Consider the example of a traditionally oriented Muslim woman who immigrated to the United States, where her daughter then grew up as an American. The client was angry with her daughter, who, contrary to the cultural tradition of arranged marriage, informed her mother that she was intending to marry a man she had met online. The therapist initially wondered if she should use cognitive restructuring to change the client's beliefs about marriage. However, after a consultation and additional information that confirmed that the woman was firm in her beliefs about marriage, the therapist helped the client learn communication skills to improve her interactions with her daughter and reshape anger-fueling thoughts to more calming but realistic ones.

Consider the case of Ajit and the culturally based belief he stated in his initial session that a son is only successful if he surpasses his father. If this belief contributed to Ajit's emotional pain, but he was not interested in reconsidering it, the therapist would not want to push on the belief. A more useful approach would be to target behavioral or environmental changes (e.g., via relaxation exercises, self-care activities, increased involvement with people who are supportive regardless of his accomplishments), or to evaluate related thoughts and beliefs that he might reconsider such as the belief that "My parents will be ashamed of me if I don't surpass my father professionally" or "I'm a failure if I'm not successful like my father." These beliefs could be probed with questions such as "How does your culture define a successful human being? Are there a variety of definitions in your culture, depending on the particular group? How is an Indian man's success defined if he does not have an identifiable father? Is there anyone in your culture you admire and consider a successful human being who did not surpass their father by profession/income/social status?" Following these questions, the utility or helpfulness of the original beliefs might be reconsidered.

RECOGNIZING AND USING CULTURAL STRENGTHS

Cognitive restructuring involves helps clients to recognize their strengths, which can be incorporated into empowering self-talk. However, in some Asian and Native cultures, it is considered arrogant and boastful to name one's own strengths. One way around this dilemma is to ask clients what the important, caring people in their lives would say. Examples include "What would your mother say she loves about you? What would your favorite teacher say is your best quality? What does your best friend say is good about you?"

In addition to individual strengths, it is important to look for and name cultural strengths. Examples include pride in one's cultural identity; religious faith or spirituality; artistic and musical abilities; bilingual and multilingual skills; culturally related knowledge and practical skills regarding fishing, hunting, farming, using medicinal plants; culture-specific beliefs that help one cope with racism, heterosexism, and other forms of oppression; a respectful attitude toward the natural environment; commitment to helping one's own group (i.e., through social action); and wisdom from experience.

STORIES, METAPHORS, AND SAYINGS

Stories, metaphors, and sayings are used to teach and reinforce important life principles in some cultures, and they can be used as a form of self-talk and reminder of more helpful thinking. In Native cultures, stories and metaphors are used as a way of offering a potential solution without telling the listener directly what to do. Often, the story is told without any expectation of discussing or interpreting it. The listener is considered free to accept the story or not, an approach that is considered more respectful of the listener's judgment.

For example, Beau Washington, a psychologist and member of the Eastern band of Cherokee Indians explained the concept of cognitive distortions in a story about a Native man who goes to university and learns about such thoughts. In many Indian Nations, the coyote is known as the trickster because he tries to mislead people, take advantage of them, and create problems, so Washington used the metaphor of a coyote to explain cognitive distortions:

> When we believe thoughts that aren't true, it's like the coyote trickster is controlling our thoughts, creating problems that are bigger than they really are. . . . One coyote thought isn't much of a problem. A pack of coyotes will take you down. If you don't chase the coyote thought away, it brings others. When we dwell on things the coyotes start to gather, creating bigger and bigger problems. The more coyotes we have and the more we dwell on a problem, the greater the pain. It's hard to fight something we can't see. Knowing the names of the coyotes brings them out of the dark into the light. Recognizing them is our best chance of ending the darkness and pain they bring. (Washington, 2012)

Metaphors provide an important teaching tool that can be incorporated into cognitive restructuring. For example, in their work with Māori people in New Zealand, Bennett, Flett, and Babbage (2014) found metaphors and prayers related to session content to be helpful in both opening and closing sessions. The authors enlisted an advisory group of Māori people who recommended using the metaphor of a *whare* (house) to explain how thoughts contribute to feelings and behaviors. This metaphor was then developed in visual form, with the foundation of the house representing significant early experiences; the first floor, core beliefs; the second floor, intermediate assumptions or rules for living; and the roof, coping strategies (sometimes protective, sometimes not; Bennett, Flett, & Babbage, 2015). The same study also highlighted a number of helpful proverbs and sayings including, for example, *Positive feelings in your heart will enhance your self-worth; Turn your face to the sun, and the shadows will fall behind you; With your food basket and my food basket, people will thrive.*

Culturally relevant sayings can be used as a kind of balanced response that may be especially powerful because they are reinforced by the culture. There is even a saying in Spanish that reminds people of the value of sayings: *En tus apuros y afanes, escuchal los consejos de refranes*—"When you're broke and feeling blue, proverbs tell you what to do" (Chahin, Villarruel, & Viramontez, 1999). Muñoz and Mendelson (2005) described how Spanish *dichos* (sayings) could be used in cognitive restructuring, using the example of the phrase *La gota de agua labra la piedra* ("A drop of water can carve a rock") to reinforce the idea that depression can be changed gradually, thought by thought.

Alcoholics Anonymous has provided numerous sayings, many of which extend beyond substance abuse, such as, *One day at a time* and *Fake it 'til you make it*. The Serenity Prayer offers a reminder that sometimes changing one's thinking is important and at other times, changing one's behavior or the situation is better: *Grant me the serenity to accept the things I cannot change, the courage to change the things I can, and the wisdom to know the difference*. Religions are another source of culture-specific stories, metaphors, and sayings. In a Christian adaptation of rational emotive therapy, Johnson and Ridley (1992) used biblical scriptures to define "ultimate truth" that countered clients' "irrational" beliefs. For example, the belief that "I must be thoroughly competent, adequate, and achieving in all possible respects if I am to consider myself worthwhile" was disputed by Isaiah 64:6: "All of us have become like one who is unclean and all our righteous acts are like filthy rags" (p. 225).

Expressive and Creative Arts Therapies

The creative arts offer an important avenue for expression, and their incorporation into CBT can reinforce the client's culture as a source of strength and support. For example, drawing was used as an avenue for storytelling that pulled parents and children closer in a group therapy program with Aboriginal Australians, and it empowered parents to recognize their own personal resources (Stock, Mares, & Robinson, 2012). Such approaches can also help clients who have limited language proficiency, a speech disability, and those who are less verbally oriented.

Malchiodi and Rozum (2012) described three ways in which visual art can be used nonverbally for cognitive restructuring. The client may be asked to "create an image" of the depression, anxiety, anger, or other emotions (using the particular phrase "create an image" rather than "art" or "draw" because the latter terms may be intimidating). Second, the client can create an image of "How I can prepare for a stressor," or "Step-by-step management of the problem." For example, after one client drew an image illustrating how much she hated her body, she then took the same drawing and added her husband's arms lovingly wrapped around her body. Third, image making can be used for stress reduction and to make meaning out of one's experiences. For example, collecting photos from magazines can be a precursor to the creation of a visual journal or a positive intention board.

In their work with transgender people, Craig, McInroy, Alloggia, and McCready (2014) described their use of a "Trans-Affirmative Hope Box" filled with inspiring and affirming items, such as a genderqueer pride button, favorite lyrics, poems, a list of goals, photos of caring people, and symbols of safe and joyful places such as the LGBTQ community center. This idea can be further developed into a Virtual Hope Box cocreated by the client and clinician working together (available as a smartphone app and clinician's manual; Austin & Craig, 2015; see http://t2health.dcoe. mil/products/mobile-apps), and idea that was originally inspired by cognitive behavioral work geared toward instilling hope in suicidal clients (Brown et al., 2005; Wenzel, Brown, & Beck, 2009).

Expressive and creative approaches can be especially helpful to facilitate cognitive change with children. For example, an evidence-based approach known as trauma-focused CBT was adapted for work with American Indian children in a program called *Honoring Children, Mending the Circle*. This program incorporates CBT concepts that parallel traditional beliefs and practices (BigFoot & Schmidt, 2010), such as traditional healers' instructions at ceremonies and activities to "leave bad thoughts at the door" or "come in with good thoughts" (BigFoot & Braden, 2007, p. 21). Chorpita (2007) also described an evidence-based protocol for obsessive–compulsive disorder and anxiety disorders with children, which had its basis in effectiveness with culturally diverse families in Hawaii. Glickman (2009) used an adaptation in which hundreds of specially developed pictures facilitated the teaching and development of psychosocial skills for children and adults with language and learning challenges (including deaf children).

Homework

Culture can affect homework in a number of ways. For one, the cultural context may limit available homework options. For example, Paradis, Cukor, and Friedman (2006) described the need for homework with Orthodox Jewish clients living in close communities to be especially discrete because even the inference that a person might be experiencing a mental health problem could affect the marriage prospects of that individual or a family member. On the other hand, cultural values and practices may facilitate the performance of homework, as in the example of Chinese immigrant clients in Australia, whose cultural philosophies and values—of self-improvement, hard work, respect for education and authority, and desire to protect the family's reputation by doing well—contributed to high levels of adherence to homework assignments (Foo & Kazantzis, 2007).

Culture influences the types of homework clients prefer. For example, in her work with an older Chinese man, one therapist used the Older Person's Pleasant Events Schedule (Gallagher & Thompson, 1981) to obtain the client's report of enjoyable activities, some of which the client subsequently agreed to do as homework. However, the client did not follow through until the therapist asked him to develop his own list (which consisted of tai chi, Chinese calligraphy, walking, reading the Chinese newspaper, and visiting Chinatown), for which his compliance was 100% (A. W. Lau & Kinoshita, 2006). This case study illustrates the importance of cultural relevance and ensuring that clients agree to activities they truly want to do and not simply out of deference to the therapist. Toward this end, asking clients to develop their own homework often solves this problem. A helpful question may be: "Based on what we talked about and did today, what is the smallest possible step you could take that would help you feel like you are making progress/healing/achieving your goals?" (Dolan, 1991). Emphasis is placed on the smallest step because change is difficult, and a small step increases the likelihood of adherence.

In some cases, the idea of homework will be off-putting because it feels like school, and school may have been a punishing experience (e.g., for many people living in generational poverty) or because it feels too formal and impersonal (e.g., older Native clients). Whatever the case, a collaborative approach is essential because it communicates the therapist's respect for the client's assessment of their own needs and strengths given their particular context. Sometimes simply using a different word may be helpful, for example, the terms *practice*, *activity*, or *mission* instead of homework. Or the homework may be something as simple as asking the client to just "think about what we talked about today and tell me your thoughts about it next time."

Conclusion

Historically, CBT assumed a dominant cultural perspective, but such assumptions are changing as researchers, teachers, therapists, and clients become more diverse and increasing attention is given to cultural influences. The increasingly international scope of CBT demands that theorists and therapists examine its multicultural nature and application (Naeem & Kingdon, 2012). Fortunately, CBT's flexibility and eclectic orientation make it particularly well suited for multicultural use. At the same time, recognition of CBT's limitations offers opportunities for expanding and refining its practice.

Conclusion

T his final chapter briefly highlights some of the current issues in the field of cognitive behavioral therapy (CBT). It is hoped that the identification and brief discussion of these issues will help the reader to have a broader context to understand both the current state of the field of CBT and some of its potential future trajectories. Of course, the field continues to evolve, and so interested practitioners will need to engage in ongoing training and upgrading, as discussed in this Conclusion.

Manualized and Transdiagnostic CBT

As was noted in the Introduction to this volume, the early history of CBT involved the development and validation of a number of specific treatment programs for relatively discrete disorders and problems. Because the techniques of CBT

http://dx.doi.org/10.1037/14936-009
Cognitive Behavioral Therapy Techniques and Strategies, by A. Wenzel, K. S. Dobson, and P. A. Hays

were specified fairly precisely and because the treatment protocols were written with a specified number of sessions and with a reasonably predictable sequence of interventions, the field advanced rapidly. The development of treatment manuals also enabled the training of new therapists to practice in a way that was consistent with the manuals, as well as a commensurate development of treatment fidelity assessment methods (McGlinchey & Dobson, 2003).

Although the development of treatment manuals was a significant benefit for research in the field of CBT, this approach was not without its detractors. Concerns were raised about the large emphasis in CBT on treatment methods and techniques, and as a counterresponse some authors went so far as to claim that the outcomes of CBT are based on nonspecific therapeutic relationship factors or the common characteristics in psychotherapy (Howard, Lueger, Maling, & Martinovich, 1993). As we have attempted to demonstrate throughout the current volume, however, cognitive behavioral therapists continually monitor the therapeutic relationship, provide education to the client about the wide range of ideas and methods that are being considered in treatment, incorporate direct client feedback in the development and use of various strategies, and generally attend to the client's response to the treatment as it unfolds. Cognitive behavioral theorists will therefore argue that the therapeutic relationship is an essential ingredient of effective therapy but that it is not sufficient because treatment techniques need to also be used within the context of an effective therapeutic relationship to attain maximal treatment outcomes.

There is little doubt that some specific techniques are required for the efficacious treatment of certain specific disorders. For example, exposure-based methods are an integral aspect of the effective treatment of a wide range of specific and social anxiety disorders, and we suggest that no credible therapist would argue that a specific anxiety disorder has been adequately resolved unless the client can approach the feared object or refrain from escaping that object if he or she has contact with it. As another example, most cognitive behavioral therapists would argue that improved affect regulation is an integral skill for the treatment of borderline personality disorder and that without the development and proper utilization of this skill, treatment has not been fully implemented (Linehan, 2015). These points being noted, there is an emphasis in the field on treatment models and methods that cut across specific diagnostic conditions and that may in their own right serve as a necessary and sufficient treatment model for most forms of mental health disorders. This move toward transdiagnostic CBT (Farchione et al., 2012) is relatively recent, however, and the extent to which transdiagnostic approaches as opposed to diagnosis specific treatment models and methods will ultimately be of maximal clinical utility remains for future determination.

The Movement Toward Evidence-Based Practice

As with the field of evidence-based medicine in general, the field of psychotherapy is moving rapidly toward the promotion of evidence-based treatments (Layard & Clark, 2014). Although CBT has a significant and growing database to support its general efficacy, it must be noted that CBT is not alone in the field of treatments that have evidence to support them. Furthermore, there is now ample evidence that some nonspecific treatment factors (e.g., the therapeutic alliance, homework, psychoeducation) have an important role to play in a fully understood evidence-based psychotherapy process.

Despite the large and growing amount of research in the field of CBT, no single comprehensive model for the integration of evidence-based psychotherapy factors and specific treatment techniques yet exists, either for specific disorders or for the field in general. Many contemporary texts—this one included—emphasize the importance of a multifaceted and multidimensional assessment of clients to promote a case conceptualization that is comprehensive and explanatory of the client's presenting problems and that can provide direction for the therapy process. Although case conceptualizations draw on our general or nomothetic understanding of disorders and common problems, they must be applied ideographically with each specific client. In many respects, we argue that the "art" of CBT lies in the ability of the cognitive behavioral therapist to integrate all of the information about the client, including the moment-by-moment experiences in the therapy room, to create an environment in which change can be contemplated, personal risks can be taken, and novel insights about one's self and one's relationship to the world can be explored through cognitive and behavioral change.

It remains to be seen to what extent the field of CBT can be truly evidence based. When we consider the wide range of human behavior and the spectacular variability in the ways that individuals think about the world and themselves (both with an individual at a particular period of time and across the lifespan), it is difficult to imagine that any one prescriptive set of principles can be generated and applied universally in psychotherapy. Nonetheless, to the extent that CBT is at the forefront of the movement toward evidence-based practice in psychotherapy, we encourage further study of both the mechanisms of change and ways to improve therapeutic outcome. We know, for example, that not everyone who enters CBT will complete the treatment (i.e., there is dropout, both due to client dissatisfaction with the treatment and mismatch between the client's problems and the potential solutions offered by CBT) and even that all clients who do complete a fulsome course of therapy may not fully improve. Thus, although the field has made substantial gains, there remains much to do to derive and utilize the best possible evidence in clinical decision making.

Evolution and Adaptation of CBT

Creativity and innovation are two of the hallmark features of human beings. We rarely stop to appreciate what we have and often instead imagine what "could be" and move in that direction. So it is in the field of psychotherapy. Early behavioral approaches to psychotherapy evolved into CBT in the 1970s and 1980s, and even the field of CBT has significantly evolved in terms of the breadth and scope of treatment models (K. S. Dobson, 2009). Often, the research basis for any particular treatment model or manual had barely been developed before the manual itself was adapted and applied to new and, in some cases, unforeseen areas of practice.

Perhaps the largest recent innovation in the field of CBT has been what is sometimes termed the *third wave* (Hayes, 2004; Hayes, Luoma, Bond, Masuda, & Lillis, 2006). This adaptation includes models and methods based on Eastern philosophies and includes such ideas as the incorporation of mindfulness-based practices into CBT, self-compassion, positive psychology, and the idea of acceptance as a therapy principle. "Third-wave" and acceptance-oriented principles have been incorporated into comprehensive treatments for such conditions as depression (Segal, Williams, & Teasdale, 2013), borderline personality disorder (Linehan, 2015), couples therapy (Jacobson & Christensen, 1998), and a variety of other conditions. Furthermore, some of these principles are being used both in the treatment of acute disorders and increasingly as preventive strategies that can promote resiliency and reduce the long-term risk of future disorder and dysfunction.

Some theorists argue that the third-wave ideas are entirely compatible with the broader field of CBT (Hofmann, Sawyer, & Fang, 2010), whereas others suggest that the dominant CBT models themselves need to be adapted to reflect the newer ideas and principles incorporated in the third wave (Hayes, 2004). At present, it remains unclear whether the third-wave ideas can or cannot be adequately accommodated within a broader CBT framework, and, if they are accommodated, to what extent they may improve treatment outcomes or the number of clients who respond to CBT (Öst, 2008). Nonetheless, mindfulness, compassion-based, and acceptance-oriented interventions are extremely popular within the

CBT movement, and there is no doubt that these ideas and principles will continue to influence the field for some time to come. As such, readers of this volume are encouraged to watch this development and to consider the judicious use of both change and acceptance oriented practices within their own cognitive behavioral therapy work.

Training and Credentialing

Given the significant attention paid to CBT in the field of psychotherapy and the focus on evidence-based treatments in health care, it is not surprising that there is an enormous demand for graduate and professional training in the field. Furthermore, programs such as the Improving Access to Psychological Therapies (Clark, 2011) in England and the federal funding of CBT in Australia have spurred the interest for retraining into CBT from a large number of existing practitioners. As a consequence, professional training programs, licensing bodies, and health care systems more generally all have a vested interest in the design and development of optimal training programs for CBT.

Beyond the graduate and professional level training and retraining programs, there has been a significant movement toward credentialing within the field of CBT. This process has been spurred in part by the desire to promote optimal training standards and quality of care and in part due to concerns that some individuals who are not properly trained and credentialed might claim unwarranted expertise in CBT. Several national organizations now offer credentials in CBT (e.g., the British Association for Behavioural & Cognitive Psychotherapies: http://www.babcp.com; The Canadian Association of Cognitive and Behavioural Therapies: http://www.cacbt.ca), several developers of specific treatment models have developed credentialing systems (eye movement desensitization and reprocessing therapy: http://www.emdr.com; and dialectical behavior therapy: http://www.behavioraltech.org), and there also exist not-for-profit independent and generic credentialing organizations for CBT (e.g., the Academy of Cognitive Therapy: http://www.academyofct.org). All of these training and credentialing organizations encourage a combination of didactic education, workshop or other facilitated learning (e.g., videos), and case work with supervised practice as the optimal method to obtain competence in the field of CBT. What varies dramatically among these various credentialing organizations, however, is the content and intensity of the training experience. Thus, some training models for relatively focused interventions can include a relatively modest amount of training or retraining, whereas other credentials require extensive education and supervision.

In summary, although there is a broad consensus about the need for training to provide high-quality CBT, there is relatively little agreement regarding the optimal method to train treatment fidelity within the field of CBT. Our argument is that, generally speaking, cognitive behavioral therapists should belong to an organization that provides a professional license in their state or national jurisdiction and that, ideally, they should hold certification from the relevant state or national credentialing organization for CBT. We anticipate that as the field matures, an emerging consensus on the nature of optimal training will develop, but for the sake of our clients, we encourage the readers of this volume to obtain the best possible training that they can in their locale before they provide services.

Dissemination Issues

As the field of CBT evolves and a larger number of evidence-based approaches to the treatment of mental and physical disorders emerges, it can be expected that the popular demand for treatment will increase. Some countries have already recognized the disjuncture between the demand for evidence-based psychotherapies and the number of available trained practitioners. The responses to this mismatch have varied. In some countries, significant amounts of time, energy, and resources have been put into training (e.g., England). In others, increased funding has been provided to attract existing practitioners to the field (e.g., Australia, Germany). At times, enhanced credentialing and status have been awarded to practitioners who hold specific credentials.

Yet another notable development in the field of CBT has been the dissemination of treatments through technology. Internet-based cognitive behavioral treatments are now relatively common, and mobile technologies, handheld device applications (apps), and telephone and Internet communication devices are regularly employed for the delivery of CBT. It has been argued that there will never be enough trained practitioners to provide individual CBT for the number of people who would benefit from this service, and so the only reasonable strategy is to use technology to provide the widest possible exposure of evidence-based treatments to the public at large.

The research evidence generally supports that Internet-based therapies can be as effective as individual therapy (Andersson & Titov, 2014; Andrews & Titov, 2009) but that there are some limits to their application. For example, it appears that Internet-alone treatments do not have the same success as facilitated or therapist-assisted Internet-based therapies for the treatment of depression (Titov et al., 2010). Thus, at least in the treatment of depression, some level of human contact or accountability appears to be needed for the treatments to be fully used by clients and to have maximum impact. The extent to which Internet and computerized systems can be made to be attractive and to encourage the completion of online or application-based interventions is a matter of ongoing research and technology development. If the developers of these technological approaches to the delivery of CBT are successful and if the outcomes of these innovative delivery mechanisms can approximate those of more traditional face-to-face delivery of CBT, it is possible that the face-to-face CBT will become less important over time. Such a development will take some years to occur, no doubt, and there will undoubtedly be some resistance to this idea from both CBT practitioners and members of the public who consider psychotherapy to be in interpersonal process. The future will tell what direction and how far this approach may take.

Another issue with respect to dissemination is its broad applicability across different cultures and diversity contexts. It has been noted that many of the original developers of CBT come from Western societies (Naeem, Swelam, & Kingdon, 2012). As such, it is appropriate to question the extent to which these therapies can be meaningfully and successfully applied to cultural groups within Western society or to other cultural groups around the globe. In this volume, we have emphasized the importance of contextual factors in the delivery of CBT. No doubt, the issue of whether cognitive behavioral therapies can simply be transported from one culture to another, or the extent to which cultural adaptation is necessary, will be an important and continuing discussion in the field of CBT. We also note that this particular issue may interface with the use of technology as a dissemination strategy. Although technology can be applied broadly (even globally), the adaptation of technological solutions is relatively difficult to make. Given this circumstance, it is possible that people in one part of the world may use technologies that were developed in other parts of the world but that are not culturally or contextually appropriate, and so the outcomes may be relatively weak or nonexistent. We therefore encourage people who develop Internet and other technology-based dissemination strategies for CBT, to the extent possible, to monitor outcomes in various parts of the world to see to what extent cultural context may matter.

The Future of CBT

As we have tried to portray throughout this volume, CBT has many positive features that recommend it as a model of psychotherapy. It is a clinically rich, personally meaningful, and highly adaptive form of treatment that can be applied in a clinically sensitive manner with people from a broad array of backgrounds and cultures. As the cases in this book have demonstrated, the model can be used for a wide range of presenting problems and relationship issues that emerge in the course of psychotherapy. The evidence base for CBT is strong, even though there are areas that require further evaluation as the field continues to expand and grow, and the treatment model is being generally integrated into the evolution of evidence-based practice. Significant attention has been paid to CBT in many corners of the world, and in some cases, significant national resources have been dedicated to the training of therapists and the broader dissemination of cognitive behavioral therapies.

In short, the field of CBT is possibly at its zenith. Of course, it is always hazardous to make future predictions, and so although this chapter ventures some relatively safe predictions about the near future, we refrain from wild speculation about distant prospects. We encourage interested readers to learn more about CBT, particularly if they have specific treatment interests or if any of the ideas in this book have spurred their desire for more knowledge about particular content areas. We also encourage interested readers to consider consulting the companion DVD series, published by the American Psychological Association, which generally follows the same order of content as the chapters in the current volume. Together, we believe that this book and the companion DVDs make an excellent set of training materials, and we hope that the information in these resources will be of value to novice and experienced cognitive behavioral therapists alike.

References

Abramowitz, J. S., Deacon, B. J., & Whiteside, S. P. H. (2011). *Exposure therapy for anxiety: Principles and practice.* New York, NY: Guilford Press.

Achenbach, T. M. (1991/2001). *Child Behavior Checklist—Cross-Informant Version.* Burlington, VT: Author.

Achenbach, T. M. (2001). *Manual for the Teacher Report Form and the Child Behavior Profile.* Burlington, VT: Author.

Alford, B. A., & Beck, A. T. (1997a). *The integrative power of cognitive therapy.* New York, NY: Guilford Press.

Alford, B. A., & Beck, A. T. (1997b). The relation of psychotherapy integration to established systems of psychotherapy. *Journal of Psychotherapy Integration, 7,* 275–289. http://dx.doi.org/10.1023/B:JOPI.0000010884.36432.0b

American Psychiatric Association. (1980). *Diagnostic and statistical manual of mental disorders* (3rd ed.). Washington, DC: Author.

American Psychological Association. (2003). Guidelines on multicultural education, training, research, practice, and organizational change for psychologists. *American Psychologist, 58,* 377–402.

Andersson, G., & Titov, N. (2014). Advantages and limitations of Internet-based interventions for common mental disorders. *World Psychiatry, 13,* 4–11. http://dx.doi.org/10.1002/wps.20083

Andrews, G., & Titov, N. (2009). Hit and miss: Innovation and the dissemination of evidence based psychological treatments. *Behaviour Research and Therapy, 47,* 974–979. http://dx.doi.org/10.1016/j.brat.2009.07.007

APA Presidential Task Force on Evidence-Based Practice. (2006). Evidence-based practice in psychology. *American Psychologist, 61,* 271–285.

Arredondo, P., & Pérez, P. (2006). Historical perspectives on the multicultural guidelines and contemporary applications. *Professional Psychology: Research and Practice, 37,* 1–5. http://dx.doi.org/10.1037/0735-7028.37.1.1

Austin, A., & Craig, S. L. (2015). Transgender affirmative cognitive behavioral therapy: Clinical considerations and applications. *Professional Psychology: Research and Practice, 46,* 21–29. http://dx.doi.org/10.1037/a0038642

Bandura, A. (1986). *Social foundations of thought and action: A social cognitive therapy.* Englewood Cliffs, NJ: Prentice-Hall.

Barker, C. H., Cook, K. L., & Borrego, J., Jr. (2010). Addressing cultural variables in parent training programs with Latino families. *Cognitive and Behavioral Practice, 17,* 157–166. http://dx.doi.org/10.1016/j.cbpra.2010.01.002

Barlow, D. H., Farchione, T. J., Fairholme, C. P., Ellard, K. K., Boisseau, C. L., Allen, L. B., & Ehrenreich-May, J. (2011). *Unified protocol for transdiagnostic treatment of emotional disorders: Therapist guide.* New York, NY: Oxford University Press.

Basilio, C. D., Knight, G. P., O'Donnell, M., Roosa, M. W., Gonzales, N. A., Umaña-Taylor, A. J., & Torres, M. (2014). The Mexican American biculturalism scale: Bicultural comfort, facility, and advantages for adolescents and adults. *Psychological Assessment, 26,* 539–554. http://dx.doi.org/10.1037/a0035951

Beck, A. T. (1970). Cognitive therapy: Nature and relation to behavior therapy. *Behavior Therapy, 1,* 184–200. http://dx.doi.org/10.1016/S0005-7894(70)80030-2

Beck, A. T., Rush, A. J., Shaw, B. F., & Emery, G. (1979). *Cognitive therapy of depression.* New York, NY: Guilford Press.

Beck, A. T., & Steer, R. A. (1988). *Manual for the Beck Hopelessness Scale.* San Antonio, TX: The Psychological Corporation.

Beck, A. T., & Steer, R. A. (1990). *Beck Anxiety Inventory Manual.* San Antonio, TX: The Psychological Corporation.

Beck, A. T., Steer, R. A., & Brown, G. K. (1996). *Manual for Beck Depression Inventory—II.* San Antonio, TX: The Psychological Corporation.

Beck, J. S. (2005). *Cognitive therapy for challenging problems: What to do when the basics don't work.* New York, NY: Guilford Press.

Beck, J. S. (2011). *Cognitive behavior therapy: Basics and beyond* (2nd ed.). New York, NY: Guilford Press.

Benish, S. G., Quintana, S., & Wampold, B. E. (2011). Culturally adapted psychotherapy and the legitimacy of myth: A direct-comparison meta-analysis. *Journal of Counseling Psychology, 58,* 279–289. http://dx.doi.org/10.1037/a0023626

Bennett, S. T., Flett, R. A., & Babbage, D. R. (2014). Culturally adapted cognitive behaviour therapy for Māori with major depression. *The Cognitive Behaviour Therapist, 7,* 1–16.

Bennett, S. T., Flett, R. A., & Babbage, D. R. (2015). *Considerations for the delivery of culturally competent cognitive-behavioral therapy for depression with Māori.* Unpublished manuscript, School of Psychology, Massey University, Wellington, New Zealand.

BigFoot, D. S., & Braden, J. (2007, Winter). Adapting evidence-based treatments for use with American Indian and Native Alaskan children and youth. *Focal Point, 21*(1), 19–22. Retrieved from http://www.icctc.org/focus%20article.pdf

BigFoot, D. S., & Schmidt, S. R. (2010). Honoring children, mending the circle: Cultural adaptation of trauma-focused cognitive behavioral therapy for American Indian and Alaska Native children. *Journal of Clinical Psychology, 66,* 847–856. http://dx.doi.org/10.1002/jclp.20707

Braun, J. D., Strunk, D. R., Sasso, K. E., & Cooper, A. A. (2015). Therapist use of Socratic questioning predicts session-to-session symptom change in cognitive therapy for depression. *Behaviour Research and Therapy, 70,* 32–37.

Brown, G. K., Ten Have, T., Henriques, G. R., Xie, S. X., Hollander, J. E., & Beck, A. T. (2005). Cognitive therapy for the prevention of suicide attempts: A randomized controlled trial. *JAMA, 294,* 563–570. http://dx.doi.org/10.1001/jama.294.5.563

Burns, D. D. (1980). *Feeling good: The new mood therapy.* New York, NY: Signet.

Castonguay, L. E., & Beutler, L. E. (Eds.). (2006). *Principles of therapeutic change that work.* New York, NY: Oxford University Press.

Cayoun, B. A. (2011). *Mindfulness-integrated CBT: Principles and practice.* http://dx.doi.org/10.1002/9781119993162

Chahin, J., Villarruel, F. A., & Viramontez, R. A. (1999). *Dichos* and *refranes*: The transmission of cultural values and beliefs. In H. Pipes McAdoo (Ed.), *Family ethnicity: Strength in diversity* (pp. 153–167). Thousand Oaks, CA: Sage.

Chambless, D. L., Sanderson, W. C., Shoham, V., Bennett Johnson, S., Pope, K. S., Crits-Christoph, P., . . . McCurry, S. (1996). An update on empirically validated therapies. *The Clinical Psychologist, 49,* 5–18.

Chorpita, B. (2007). *Modular cognitive-behavioral therapy for childhood anxiety disorders.* New York, NY: Guilford Press.

Clark, D. M. (2011). Implementing NICE guidelines for the psychological treatment of depression and anxiety disorders: The IAPT experience. *International Review of Psychiatry, 23*, 318–327. http://dx.doi.org/10.3109/09540261.2011.606803

Clore, G. L., & Ortony, A. (2000). Cognition in emotion: Always, sometimes, or never. In R. D. R. Lane, L. Nadel, G. L. Ahern, J. Allen, & A. W. Kasniak (Eds.), *Cognitive neuroscience of emotion* (pp. 24–61). New York, NY: Oxford University Press.

Comas-Díaz, L., & Duncan, J. W. (1985). The cultural context: A factor in assertiveness training with mainland Puerto Rican women. *Psychology of Women Quarterly, 9*, 463–476. http://dx.doi.org/10.1111/j.1471-6402.1985.tb00896.x

Cowan, M. J., Freedland, K. E., Burg, M. M., Saab, P. G., Youngblood, M. E., Cornell, C. E., . . . Czajkowski, S. M. (2008). Predictors of treatment response for depression and inadequate social support—The ENRICHD randomized clinical trial. *Psychotherapy and Psychosomatics, 77*, 27–37. http://dx.doi.org/10.1159/000110057

Craig, S. L., McInroy, L., Alloggia, R., & McCready, L. (2014). Like picking up a seed, but you haven't planted it: Queer youth analyze the It Gets Better Project. *International Journal of Child, Youth, and Family Studies, 1*, 204–219.

Craske, M. G., Kircanski, K., Zelikowsky, M., Mystkowski, J., Chowdhury, N., & Baker, A. (2008). Optimizing inhibitory learning during exposure therapy. *Behaviour Research and Therapy, 46*, 5–27. http://dx.doi.org/10.1016/j.brat.2007.10.003

Craske, M. G., Treanor, M., Conway, C. C., Zbozinek, T., & Vervliet, B. (2014). Maximizing exposure therapy: An inhibitory learning approach. *Behaviour Research and Therapy, 58*, 10–23. http://dx.doi.org/10.1016/j.brat.2014.04.006

DeRubeis, R. J., Brotman, M. A., & Gibbons, C. J. (2005). A conceptual and methodological analysis of the nonspecific argument. *Clinical Psychology: Science and Practice, 12*, 174–183. http://dx.doi.org/10.1093/clipsy.bpi022

DeRubeis, R. J., & Feeley, M. (1990). Determinants of change in cognitive therapy for depression. *Cognitive Therapy and Research, 14*, 469–482. http://dx.doi.org/10.1007/BF01172968

Dimidjian, S., Hollon, S. D., Dobson, K. S., Schmaling, K. B., Kohlenberg, R. J., Addis, M. E., . . . Jacobson, N. S. (2006). Randomized trial of behavioral activation, cognitive therapy, and antidepressant medication in the acute treatment of adults with major depression. *Journal of Consulting and Clinical Psychology, 74*, 658–670. http://dx.doi.org/10.1037/0022-006X.74.4.658

Dobson, D., & Dobson, K. S. (2009). *Evidence-based practice of cognitive-behavioral therapy.* New York, NY: Guilford Press.

Dobson, K. S. (Ed.). (2009). *Handbook of cognitive-behavioral therapies* (3rd ed.). New York, NY: Guilford Press.

Dobson, K. S., & Dozois, D. J. A. (2009). Historical and philosophical bases of the cognitive-behavioral therapies. *Handbook of cognitive-behavioral therapies* (3rd ed., pp. 3–38). New York, NY: Guilford Press.

Dolan, Y. M. (1991). *Resolving sexual abuse.* New York, NY: Norton.

D'Zurilla, T. J., Nezu, A. M., & Maydeu-Olivares, A. (2002). *Manual for the Social Problem Solving Inventory—Revised.* North Tonawanda, NY: Multi-Health Systems.

Ellis, A., & Whiteley, M. M. (Eds.). (1979). *Theoretical and empirical foundations of rational-emotive therapy.* Monterey, CA: Brooks/Cole.

Emmelkamp, P. M., & Mersch, P. P. (1982). Cognition and exposure in vivo in the treatment of agoraphobia: Short-term and delayed effects. *Cognitive Therapy and Research, 6,* 77–90. http://dx.doi.org/10.1007/BF01185728

Epp, A. M., & Dobson, K. S. (2010). The evidence base for cognitive-behavior therapy. In K. S. Dobson (Ed.), *Handbook of cognitive-behavioral therapies* (3rd ed., pp. 39–73). New York, NY: Guilford Press.

Erickson-Schroth, L. (2014). *Trans bodies, trans selves: A resource for the transgender community.* New York, NY: Oxford University Press.

Farchione, T. J., Fairholme, C. P., Ellard, K. K., Boisseau, C. L., Thompson-Hollands, J., Carl, J. R., . . . Barlow, D. H. (2012). Unified protocol for transdiagnostic treatment of emotional disorders: A randomized controlled trial. *Behavior Therapy, 43,* 666–678. http://dx.doi.org/10.1016/j.beth.2012.01.001

Farmer, R. F., & Chapman, A. (2008). *Behavioral interventions in cognitive behavior therapy: Practical guidance for putting theory into action.* http://dx.doi.org/10.1037/11664-000

Feeley, M., DeRubeis, R. J., & Gelfand, L. A. (1999). The temporal relation of adherence and alliance to symptom change in cognitive therapy for depression. *Journal of Consulting and Clinical Psychology, 67,* 578–582. http://dx.doi.org/10.1037/0022-006X.67.4.578

Fehm, L., & Mrose, J. (2008). Patients' perspective on homework assignments in cognitive-behavioural therapy. *Clinical Psychology & Psychotherapy, 15,* 320–328. http://dx.doi.org/10.1002/cpp.592

First, M. B., Williams, J. B. W., & Spitzer, R. L. (2015). *Structured Clinical Interview for DSM–5 Disorders—Clinician Version (SCID–5–CV).* Arlington, VA: American Psychiatric Publishing.

Foa, E. B., & Kozak, M. J. (1986). Emotional processing of fear: Exposure to corrective information. *Psychological Bulletin, 99,* 20–35. http://dx.doi.org/10.1037/0033-2909.99.1.20

Foo, K. H., & Kazantzis, N. (2007). Integrating homework assignments based on culture: Working with Chinese patients. *Cognitive and Behavioral Practice, 17,* 157–166.

Gallagher, D., & Thompson, L. W. (1981). *Depression in the elderly: A behavioral treatment manual.* Los Angeles: University of Southern California Press.

Glickman, N. S. (2009). Adapting best practices in CBT for deaf and hearing persons with language and learning challenges. *Journal of Psychotherapy Integration, 19,* 354–384. http://dx.doi.org/10.1037/a0017969

Gonzalez, V. M., Schmitz, J. M., & DeLaune, K. A. (2006). The role of homework in cognitive-behavioral therapy for cocaine dependence. *Journal of Consulting and Clinical Psychology, 74,* 633–637. http://dx.doi.org/10.1037/0022-006X.74.3.633

Greenberg, L. S., McWilliams, N., & Wenzel, A. (2014). *Exploring three approaches to psychotherapy.* http://dx.doi.org/10.1037/14253-000

Hackmann, A., Bennett-Levy, J., & Holmes, E. A. (2011). *Oxford guide to imagery in cognitive therapy.* Oxford, England: Oxford University Press.

Hayes, S. C. (2004). Acceptance and commitment therapy, relational frame therapy, and the third wave of behavioural and cognitive therapies. *Behavior Therapy, 35,* 639–665. http://dx.doi.org/10.1016/S0005-7894(04)80013-3

Hayes, S. C., Luoma, J. B., Bond, F. W., Masuda, A., & Lillis, J. (2006). Acceptance and commitment therapy: Model, processes and outcomes. *Behaviour Research and Therapy, 44,* 1–25. http://dx.doi.org/10.1016/j.brat.2005.06.006

Hayes, S. C., Strosahl, K. D., & Wilson, K. G. (2011). *Acceptance and commitment therapy: The process and practice of mindful change* (2nd ed.). New York, NY: Guilford Press.

Hays, P. A. (2009). Integrating evidence-based practice, cognitive-behavior therapy, and multicultural therapy: Ten steps for culturally competent practice. *Professional Psychology: Research and Practice, 40,* 354–360. http://dx.doi.org/10.1037/a0016250

Hays, P. A. (2013). *Connecting across cultures: The helper's toolkit.* Thousand Oaks, CA: Sage.

Hays, P. A. (2014). *Creating well-being: Four steps to a happier healthier life.* http://dx.doi.org/10.1037/14317-000

Hays, P. A. (2016). *Addressing cultural complexities in practice: Assessment, diagnosis, and therapy* (3rd ed.). Washington, DC: American Psychological Association.

Hays, P. A., & Iwamasa, G. Y. (Eds.). (2006). *Culturally responsive cognitive-behavioral therapy* (pp. 179–198). Washington, DC: American Psychological Association.

Hofmann, S. G., Sawyer, A. T., & Fang, A. (2010). The empirical status of the "new wave" of cognitive behavioral therapy. *Psychiatric Clinics of North America, 33,* 701–710. http://dx.doi.org/10.1016/j.psc.2010.04.006

Holmes, E. A., Arntz, A., & Smucker, M. R. (2007). Imagery rescripting in cognitive behaviour therapy: Images, treatment techniques and outcomes. *Journal of Behavior Therapy and Experimental Psychiatry, 38,* 297–305. http://dx.doi.org/10.1016/j.jbtep.2007.10.007

Howard, K. I., Lueger, R. J., Maling, M. S., & Martinovich, Z. (1993). A phase model of psychotherapy outcome: Causal mediation of change. *Journal of Consulting and Clinical Psychology, 61,* 678–685. http://dx.doi.org/10.1037/0022-006X.61.4.678

Huey, S. J., Jr., Tilley, J. L., Jones, E. O., & Smith, C. A. (2014). The contribution of cultural competence to evidence-based care for ethnically diverse populations. *Annual Review of Clinical Psychology, 10,* 305–338. http://dx.doi.org/10.1146/annurev-clinpsy-032813-153729

Jacobson, N. S., & Christensen, A. (1998). *Acceptance and change in couple therapy: A therapists' guide to transforming relationships.* New York, NY: Norton.

Johnson, W. B., & Ridley, C. R. (1992). Brief Christian and non-Christian rational-emotive therapy with depressed Christian clients: An exploratory study. *Counseling and Values, 36,* 220–229. http://dx.doi.org/10.1002/j.2161-007X.1992.tb00790.x

Kazantzis, N., Dattilio, F., & Dobson, K. S. (in press). *The therapeutic relationship in cognitive behavior therapy.* New York, NY: Guilford Press.

Kazantzis, N., Deane, F. P., Ronan, K. R., & L'Abate, L. (Eds.). (2005). *Using homework assignments in cognitive behavior therapy.* New York, NY: Routledge.

Kazantzis, N., & L'Abate, L. (Eds.). (2007). *Handbook of homework assignments in psychotherapy: Research, practice and prevention.* http://dx.doi.org/10.1007/978-0-387-29681-4

Kazantzis, N., Whittington, C., & Dattilio, F. (2010). Meta-analysis of homework effects in cognitive and behavioral therapy: A replication and extension. *Clinical Psychology: Science and Practice, 17,* 144–156. http://dx.doi.org/10.1111/j.1468-2850.2010.01204.x

Kelly, S. (2006). Cognitive-behavioral therapy with African Americans. In P. A. Hays & G. Y. Iwamasa (Eds.), *Culturally responsive cognitive-behavioral therapy: Assessment, practice, and supervision* (pp. 97–116). http://dx.doi.org/10.1037/11433-004

Kozak, M. J., Foa, E. B., & Steketee, G. (1988). Process and outcome of exposure treatment with obsessive-compulsives: Psychophysiological indicators of emotional processing. *Behavior Therapy, 19,* 157–169. http://dx.doi.org/10.1016/S0005-7894(88)80039-X

Kuyken, W., Fothergill, C. D., Musa, M., & Chadwick, P. (2005). The reliability and quality of cognitive case formulation. *Behaviour Research and Therapy, 43,* 1187–1201. http://dx.doi.org/10.1016/j.brat.2004.08.007

Kuyken, W., Padesky, C. A., & Dudley, R. (2008). *Collaborative case conceptualization: Working effectively with clients in cognitive-behavioral therapy.* New York, NY: Guilford Press.

LaFromboise, T. D., & Rowe, W. (1983). Skills training for bicultural competence: Rationale and application. *Journal of Counseling Psychology, 30*, 589–595. http://dx.doi.org/10.1037/0022-0167.30.4.589

Lang, A. J., & Craske, M. G. (2000). Manipulations of exposure-based therapy to reduce return of fear: A replication. *Behaviour Research and Therapy, 38*, 1–12. http://dx.doi.org/10.1016/S0005-7967(99)00031-5

La Roche, M. J., D'Angelo, E., Gualdron, L., & Leavell, J. (2006). Culturally sensitive guided imagery for allocentric Latinos: A pilot study. *Psychotherapy: Theory, Research, Practice, Training, 43*, 555–560. http://dx.doi.org/10.1037/0033-3204.43.4.555

Lau, A. S. (2012). Reflections on adapting parent training for Chinese immigrants: Blind alleys, thoroughfares, and test drives. In G. Bernal & M. M. D. Rodriguez (Eds.), *Cultural adaptations: Tools for evidence-based practice with diverse populations* (pp. 133–156). Washington, DC: American Psychological Association.

Lau, A. W., & Kinoshita, L. M. (2006). Cognitive-behavioral therapy with culturally diverse older adults. In P. A. Hays & G. Y. Iwamasa (Eds.), *Culturally responsive cognitive-behavioral therapy* (pp. 179–198). http://dx.doi.org/10.1037/11433-008

Layard, R., & Clark, D. M. (2014). *Thrive: The power of evidence-based psychological therapies.* Princeton, NJ: Princeton University Press.

Leahy, R. L. (2001). *Overcoming resistance in cognitive therapy.* New York, NY: Guilford Press.

Leahy, R. L. (2015). *Emotional schema therapy.* New York, NY: Guilford Press.

Lewinsohn, P. M. (1974). A behavioral approach to depression. In R. J. Friedman & M. M. Katz (Eds.), *The psychology of depression: Contemporary theory and research* (pp. 157–185). New York, NY: Wiley.

Linehan, M. M. (2015). *DBT skills training manual* (2nd ed.). New York, NY: Guilford Press.

Macartney, S., Bishaw, A., & Fontenot, K. (2013). *Poverty rates for selected detailed race and Hispanic groups by state and place: 2007–2011* (American Community Survey Briefs ACSBR/11-17). Retrieved from http://www.census.gov/prod/2013pubs/acsbr11-17.pdf

Mahoney, M. J. (1974). *Cognition and behavior modification.* Cambridge, MA: Ballinger.

Malchiodi, C. A., & Rozum, A. L. (2012). Cognitive-behavioral and mind–body approaches. In C. Malchiodi (Ed.), *Handbook of art therapy* (2nd ed., pp. 89–102). New York, NY: Guilford Press.

Martell, C. R., Dimidjian, S., & Herman-Dunn, R. (2010). *Behavioral activation for depression: A clinician's guide.* New York, NY: Guilford Press.

Martin, D. J., Garske, J. P., & Davis, M. K. (2000). Relation of the therapeutic alliance with outcome and other variables: A meta-analytic review. *Journal of Consulting and Clinical Psychology, 68*, 438–450. http://dx.doi.org/10.1037/0022-006X.68.3.438

McClure, A. (2011). *Census reports increased poverty among people with disabilities.* Washington, DC: National Women's Law Center. Retrieved from http://www.nwlc.org/our-blog/census-reports-increased-poverty-among-people-disabilities

McGlinchey, J., & Dobson, K. S. (2003). Treatment integrity concerns in cognitive therapy for depression. *Journal of Cognitive Psychotherapy, 17,* 299–318. http://dx.doi.org/10.1891/jcop.17.4.299.52543

McHugh, R. K., & Barlow, D. H. (2010). The dissemination and implementation of evidence-based psychological treatments. A review of current efforts. *American Psychologist, 65,* 73–84. http://dx.doi.org/10.1037/a0018121

Meichenbaum, D. H. (1977). *Cognitive behavior modification.* http://dx.doi.org/10.1007/978-1-4757-9739-8

Miller, G. A. (1956). The magical number seven plus or minus two: Some limits on our capacity for processing information. *Psychological Review, 63,* 81–97. http://dx.doi.org/10.1037/h0043158

Mona, L., Romesser-Scehnet, J. M., Cameron, R. P., & Cardenas, V. (2006). Cognitive-behavioral therapy and people with disabilities. In P. A. Hays & G. Y. Iwamasa (Eds.), *Culturally responsive cognitive-behavioral therapy* (pp. 199–222). Washington, DC: American Psychological Association.

Muñoz, R. F., & Mendelson, T. (2005). Toward evidence-based interventions for diverse populations: The San Francisco General Hospital prevention and treatment manuals. *Journal of Consulting and Clinical Psychology, 73,* 790–799. http://dx.doi.org/10.1037/0022-006X.73.5.790

Naeem, F., & Kingdon, D. (Eds.). (2012). *Cognitive behaviour therapy in non-Western cultures.* New York, NY: Nova Science.

Naeem, F., Swelam, M., & Kingdon, D. (2012). Introduction: CBT and the culture. In F. Naeem & D. Kingdon (Eds.), *Cognitive behaviour therapy in non-Western cultures* (pp. 1–14). New York, NY: Nova Science.

Nathan, P. E., Stuart, S. P., & Dolan, S. L. (2000). Research on psychotherapy efficacy and effectiveness: Between Scylla and Charybdis? *Psychological Bulletin, 126,* 964–981.

Nezu, A. M., Nezu, C. M., & D'Zurilla, T. (2013). *Problem-solving therapy: A treatment manual.* New York, NY: Springer.

Norcross, J. C., & Lambert, M. J. (2011). Evidence-based therapy. In J. C. Norcross (Ed.), *Psychotherapy relationships that work* (2nd ed., pp. 2–24). http://dx.doi.org/10.1093/acprof:oso/9780199737208.003.0001

O'Donohue, W. T., & Cucciare, M. A. (Eds.). (2008). *Terminating psychotherapy: A clinician's guide.* New York, NY: Routledge.

Olatunji, B. O., Cisler, J. M., & Deacon, B. J. (2010). Efficacy of cognitive behavioral therapy for anxiety disorders: A review of meta-analytic findings. *Psychiatric Clinics of North America, 33,* 557–577. http://dx.doi.org/10.1016/j.psc.2010.04.002

Organista, K. (2006). Cognitive-behavioral therapy with Latinos and Latinas. In P. A. Hays & G. Y. Iwamasa (Eds.), *Culturally responsive cognitive-behavioral therapy: Assessment, practice, and supervision* (pp. 73–96). http://dx.doi.org/10.1037/11433-003

Öst, L. G. (2008). Efficacy of the third wave of behavioral therapies: A systematic review and meta-analysis. *Behaviour Research and Therapy, 46,* 296–321. http://dx.doi.org/10.1016/j.brat.2007.12.005

Paradis, C. M., Cukor, D., & Friedman, S. (2006). Cognitive-behavioral therapy with Orthodox Jews. In P. A. Hays & G. Y. Iwamasa (Eds.), *Culturally responsive cognitive-behavioral therapy: Assessment, practice, and supervision* (pp. 161–176). http://dx.doi.org/10.1037/11433-007

Persons, J. B. (2008). *The case formulation approach to cognitive-behavior therapy.* New York, NY: Guilford Press.

Persons, J. B., Davidson, J., & Tompkins, M. (2001). *Essential components of cognitive-behavior therapy for depression.*

Petrik, A. M., Kazantzis, N., & Hofmann, S. G. (2013). Distinguishing integrative from eclectic practice in cognitive behavioral therapies. *Psychotherapy, 50,* 392–397. http://dx.doi.org/10.1037/a0032412

Pitman, R. K., Orr, S. P., Altman, B., Longpre, R. E., Poiré, R. E., Macklin, M. L., . . . Steketee, G. S. (1996). Emotional processing and outcome of imaginal flooding therapy in Vietnam veterans with chronic posttraumatic stress disorder. *Comprehensive Psychiatry, 37,* 409–418. http://dx.doi.org/10.1016/S0010-440X(96)90024-3

Pollock, L. R., & Williams, J. M. G. (2001). Effective problem solving in suicide attempters depends on specific autobiographical recall. *Suicide and Life-Threatening Behavior, 31,* 386–396.

Propst, L. R., Ostrom, R., Watkins, P., Dean, T., & Mashburn, D. (1992). Comparative efficacy of religious and nonreligious cognitive-behavioral therapy for the treatment of clinical depression in religious individuals. *Journal of Consulting and Clinical Psychology, 60,* 94–103. http://dx.doi.org/10.1037/0022-006X.60.1.94

Rees, C. S., McEvoy, P., & Nathan, P. R. (2005). Relationship between homework completion and outcome in cognitive behaviour therapy. *Cognitive Behaviour Therapy, 34,* 242–247. http://dx.doi.org/10.1080/16506070510011548

Riley, W. T., McCormick, M. G. F., Simon, E. M., Stack, K., Pushkin, Y., Overstreet, M. M., . . . Magakian, C. (1995). Effects of alprazolam dose on the induction and habituation processes during behavioral panic induction treatment. *Journal of Anxiety Disorders, 9,* 217–227.

Saéz-Santiago, E., Bernal, G., Reyes-Rodríguez, M. L., & Bonilla-Silva, K. (2012). Development and cultural adaptation of the *Taller de Educación Psicológica para Padres y Madres* (TEPSI): Psychoeducation for parents of Latino/a adolescents with depression. In G. Bernal &

M. M. D. Rodriguez (Eds.), *Cultural adaptations: Tools for evidence-based practice with diverse populations* (pp. 91–112). http://dx.doi.org/10.1037/13752-005

Segal, Z. V., Williams, J. M. G., & Teasdale, J. D. (2013). *Mindfulness-based cognitive therapy for depression* (2nd ed.). New York, NY: Guilford Press.

Silverman, W. K., & Albano, A. M. (2005). *Anxiety Disorders Interview Schedule (ADIS–IV) parent interview schedule.* New York, NY: Oxford University Press.

Smith, T. B., Rodríguez, M. D., & Bernal, G. (2011). Culture. *Journal of Clinical Psychology, 67,* 166–175. http://dx.doi.org/10.1002/jclp.20757

Spilka, M. J., & Dobson, K. S. (2015). Promoting the internationalization of evidence-based practice: Benchmarking as a strategy to evaluate culturally transported psychological treatments. *Clinical Psychology: Science and Practice, 22,* 58–75. http://dx.doi.org/10.1111/cpsp.12092

Stock, C., Mares, S., & Robinson, G. (2012). Telling and re-telling stories: The use of narrative and drawing in a group intervention with parents and children in a remote Aboriginal community. *Australian and New Zealand Journal of Family Therapy, 33,* 157–170. http://dx.doi.org/10.1017/aft.2012.17

Tang, T. Z., DeRubeis, R. J., Hollon, S. D., Amsterdam, J., & Shelton, R. (2007). Sudden gains in cognitive therapy of depression and depression relapse/recurrence. *Journal of Consulting and Clinical Psychology, 75,* 404–408. http://dx.doi.org/10.1037/0022-006X.75.3.404

Titov, N., Andrews, G., Davies, M., McIntyre, K., Robinson, E., & Solley, K. (2010). Internet treatment for depression: A randomized controlled trial comparing clinician vs. technician assistance. *PLoS ONE, 5,* e10939. http://dx.doi.org/10.1371/journal.pone.0010939

Trzepacz, P. T., & Baker, R. W. (1993). *The psychiatric mental status examination.* Oxford, England: Oxford University Press.

Wade, W. A., Treat, T. A., & Stuart, G. L. (1998). Transporting an empirically supported treatment for panic disorder to a service clinic setting: A benchmarking strategy. *Journal of Consulting and Clinical Psychology, 66,* 231–239. http://dx.doi.org/10.1037/0022-006X.66.2.231

Washington, B. (2012). *Coyote thoughts: A Native explains mental health.* Retrieved from http://coyotethoughts.com/The_Story.html

Webb, C. A., DeRubeis, R. J., Amsterdam, J. D., Shelton, R. C., Hollon, S. D., & Dimidjian, S. (2011). Two aspects of the therapeutic alliance: Differential relations with depressive symptom change. *Journal of Consulting and Clinical Psychology, 79,* 279–283. http://dx.doi.org/10.1037/a0023252

Webb, C. A., DeRubeis, R. J., & Barber, J. P. (2010). Therapist adherence/competence and treatment outcome: A meta-analytic review. *Journal of Consulting and Clinical Psychology, 78,* 200–211. http://dx.doi.org/ 10.1037/a0018912

Weersing, V. R., & Weisz, J. R. (2002). Community clinic treatment of depressed youth: Benchmarking usual care against CBT clinical trials. *Journal of Consulting and Clinical Psychology, 70,* 299–310. http://dx.doi. org/10.1037/0022-006X.70.2.299

Wenzel, A. (2012). Modification of core beliefs in cognitive therapy. In I. R. de Oliveira (Ed.), *Cognitive behavioral therapy* (pp. 17–34). http:// dx.doi.org/10.5772/30119

Wenzel, A. (2013). *Strategic decision making in cognitive behavioral therapy.* http://dx.doi.org/10.1037/14188-000

Wenzel, A., Brown, G. K., & Beck, A. T. (2009). *Cognitive therapy for suicidal patients: Scientific and clinical applications.* http://dx.doi.org/ 10.1037/11862-000

Westra, H. A., Dozois, D. J. A., & Marcus, M. (2007). Expectancy, homework compliance, and initial change in cognitive-behavioral therapy for anxiety. *Journal of Consulting and Clinical Psychology, 75,* 363–373. http://dx.doi.org/10.1037/0022-006X.75.3.363

Williams, J. M. G., Barnhofer, T., Crane, C., Herman, D., Raes, F., Watkins, E., & Dalgleish, T. (2007). Autobiographical memory specificity and emotional disorder. *Psychological Bulletin, 133,* 122–148. http:// dx.doi.org/10.1037/0033-2909.133.1.122

Young, J. E., Klosko, J. S., & Weishaar, M. E. (2003). *Schema therapy: A practitioner's guide.* New York, NY: Guilford Press.

Index

About the Authors

Amy Wenzel, PhD, ABPP, is owner and president of Wenzel Consulting, LLC; clinical assistant professor of psychology in psychiatry at the University of Pennsylvania School of Medicine; and an adjunct faculty member at the Beck Institute for Cognitive Behavior Therapy. She is also certified as a trainer-consultant with the Academy of Cognitive Therapy. Dr. Wenzel is author or editor of 17 books, including the *Oxford Handbook of Perinatal Psychology* (2016), *Cognitive Behavioral Therapy for Perinatal Distress* (2015), *Strategic Decision Making in Cognitive Behavioral Therapy* (2013), *Group Cognitive Therapy for Addictions* (2012; with B. S. Liese, A. T. Beck, & D. Friedman-Wheeler), and *Cognitive Therapy for Suicidal Patients: Scientific and Clinical Applications* (2009; with G. K. Brown & A. T. Beck). Dr. Wenzel has published more than 100 peer-reviewed journal articles and book chapters, and her research has been funded by the National Institutes of Health, the American Foundation for Suicide Prevention, and the National Alliance for Research on Schizophrenia and Depression (now the Brain and Behavior Foundation). She lectures internationally on cognitive behavioral therapy and has provided intensive supervision to more than 160 clinicians who have acquired competency to deliver this treatment. Dr. Wenzel has served as the featured therapist in three psychotherapy demonstration DVD series produced by the American Psychological Association. She currently divides her time among scholarly writing, training and consultation, and clinical practice. For more information on her clinical practice, publications, videos, and workshops, visit her website (http://www.dramywenzel.com).

Keith S. Dobson, PhD, is a professor of clinical psychology at the University of Calgary in Canada, where he has also served as head of psychology and director of the clinical psychology program. His research has focused on both cognitive models and mechanisms in depression as well as the treatment and prevention of relapse of depression, particularly using cognitive behavioral therapies. Dr. Dobson's research has resulted in more than 200 published articles and chapters, 12 books, and numerous conference and workshop presentations in many countries. His books include *Evidence-Based Practice of Cognitive-Behavior Therapy* (with D. Dobson; 2nd ed., in press) and the *Handbook of Cognitive-Behavioral Therapies* (3rd ed., 2010). He has three psychotherapy demonstration DVD series and a 2012 book, *Cognitive Therapy*, published by the American Psychological Association. In addition to his research in depression, Dr. Dobson has recently been engaged in research related to the integration of evidence-based treatments in family practice. He is also a principal investigator for the Opening Minds program of the Mental Health Commission of Canada, with a focus on stigma reduction related to mental disorders in the workplace. Furthermore, he has written about developments in professional psychology and ethics and has been actively involved in organized psychology in Canada, including a term as president of the Canadian Psychological Association. He is a past president of the Academy of Cognitive Therapy and the International Association for Cognitive Psychotherapy. Among other awards, he has received both the Canadian Psychological Association's Award for Distinguished Contributions to the Profession of Psychology and the Donald O. Hebb Award for Distinguished Contributions to the Science of Psychology.

Pamela A. Hays, PhD, received her doctorate in clinical psychology from the University of Hawaii and completed a National Institute of Mental Health postdoctoral fellowship at the University of Rochester School of Medicine. She was on the graduate psychology faculty of Antioch University in Seattle, Washington, for 11 years, and in 2000, returned to her hometown on the Kenai Peninsula in Alaska, where she has worked in community mental health for the Kenaitze Tribe's Dena'ina Wellness Center, established a private practice, and served on the Board of the Alaska State Psychological Association. Her research has included work with Tunisian women in North Africa and with Vietnamese, Lao, and Cambodian people in the U.S. Dr. Hays is the coeditor of *Culturally Responsive Cognitive Behavior Therapy* (2006; with G. Y. Iwamasa) and author of several books, including *Addressing Cultural Complexities in Practice* (3rd ed., 2016) and *Creating Well-Being: Four Steps to a Happier, Healthier Life* (2014). Dr. Hays's work with clients is featured in several APA-produced DVDs. She provides consultation and teaches workshops internationally. For more information on Dr. Hays's clinical practice, publications, videos, and workshops, visit her website (http://www.drpamelahays.com).